Trapped in a
Nightmare

BEST WISHES
TO HAILEY
Cecylia Ziobro Thibault

Trapped in a Nightmare

The Story of an American Girl Growing
Up in the Nazi Slave Labor Camps

CECYLIA ZIOBRO THIBAULT,
AS TOLD TO ROBERT THIBAULT

iUniverse, Inc.
Bloomington

Trapped in a Nightmare
The Story of an American Girl Growing Up in the Nazi Slave Labor Camps

iUniverse books may be ordered through booksellers or by contacting:

iUniverse
1663 Liberty Drive
Bloomington, IN 47403
www.iuniverse.com
1-800-Authors (1-800-288-4677)

ISBN: 978-1-4620-1128-5 (pbk)
ISBN: 978-1-4620-1130-8 (clth)
ISBN: 978-1-4620-1129-2 (ebk)

Printed in the United States of America

iUniverse rev. date: 4/27/11

This book is written in memory of my mother, Maria, and for the legions of soldiers who gave their lives to save millions.

Table of Contents

ACKNOWLEDGMENTS

Many thanks to my sister, Elizabeth, for encouraging me to log my memories of the war and for her historical and literary guidance.

I also offer my thanks to her husband, Reverend Allen Schaarschmidt, for providing his church, The Blessed Hope Church of the Nazarene in Phillipsburg, New Jersey, as the first channel for sharing my story in person. The outpouring of love from him and his entire congregation was a great inspiration.

My lovely daughter, Elizabeth, arranged for me to deliver speeches to students at Hampstead and Londonderry Middle Schools and Alvirne High School in New Hampshire. To Liz, and to the faculty and students who participated, I offer my deep appreciation for allowing me to spread this story to the next generation; something that is so important to me.

Thanks to my dear friend, Helena Kopij, for insisting I document my memoirs and for her friendship throughout the years.

Thanks to Bobbie Christmas at Zebra Communications for editing the manuscript, providing encouragement, and guiding us with her years of experience.

I offer my sincere thanks to the The William Breman Jewish Heritage & Holocaust Museum in Atlanta, GA for their guidance and encouragement.

I am truly grateful to all of my brothers and sisters; especially Grace, Elizabeth, Barbara, and Lucian for their input into the manuscript as it evolved.

My daughter-in-law, Camilla, and my grandchildren, Emily and Maria, I thank you for your patience and selflessness during those many times when your husband and father was busy typing away.

Finally, to my best friend for more than fifty years—my husband, Robert. Thank you for sharing the best years of my life.

Ode to my Mama

The angels must have known
How lonely with despair I'd been.
They gave me little siblings
To call my own and make me grin.
They brought me joy and laughter
With the things they said and did.
Everyone would stop and say,
"Where did you get those beautiful kids?"
Thank you angels. Thank you Mama.

Celinka

PREFACE

When my brothers and sisters, and even my children, were young, they asked me about my life during World War II. Over the years I told them only bits and pieces. I thought they were too young to comprehend what my mother and I, along with millions of other innocent people, experienced during the war. When my siblings and children got older, I recounted the stories with the same vagueness that softened the harsh realities of all we endured. The only thing that changed was my rationale for keeping these secrets locked away. I reasoned that nothing good could come from sharing those unpleasant memories. While my logic was sound, another reason may have also been to keep from having to dredge up the physical pain and emotional distress that went along with those horrific memories.

I had put all of that behind me and began a new life after the war. The war years had long passed, and although I rarely recounted the stories, I've forgotten few details. I remember most of the names and nearly all the faces. I remember the color of the walls, the texture of the fabrics, the expressions on the faces, the deafening sounds we heard, the taste of the scraps we ate, and even the scents in the air. Still, I never intended to record my story.

I am proud of my heritage, my family, and who I am. I am a humble servant of God who has never been one to boast or brag. I've never been one to showcase myself or my accomplishments, so the idea of writing this book, as recently as a few years ago, was the farthest thought from my mind. Only now, more than half a century after the war, when I hear people dismiss the Holocaust as a fairy tale, a myth, or even an exaggeration of the facts, or when I hear people dismiss the slavery and discount the human brutality of the Nazi regime, am I compelled to speak out. And so I do speak out. I speak out for the Jewish families in Poland and throughout Europe who died a merciless death during the war. I speak out for all of the people who were forced into slave labor, like my family and me. I speak out so humanity never forgets the inhumanity of which we are capable. Finally, I speak out to remind us all about the simple lesson of forgiveness, for our own good and the good of mankind.

CHAPTER 1
IN SEARCH OF A BETTER LIFE

Every now and then, my body cringes at the clear mental images of the events we lived through during the war. The bloodied face of an innocent man, disfigured by the butt of a German rifle leveled across his teeth. The despair in my mother's eyes when she picked herself up from the ground following a beating she received at the hands of the Nazi labor camp foreman. The countless bodies we passed while making our way across the German hillsides, or the hate-filled eyes of Nazi children who bullied me for the simple pleasure of it. These are the childhood memories I'd like to forget, but they are vividly etched in my mind and impossible to erase.

My name is Cecylia Teresa Ziobro. Born into poverty and raised in Nazi Germany, I am a Polish-American by birth and a product of the Nazi slave labor camps of World War II. The move to Germany was forced upon us when I was a young child. It was quite a departure from the simple life we led in Poland. The disruption allowed little time for us to come to terms with our circumstances. How did we handle it? Like any other situation a person encounters. We simply handled each event as it came. I'm probably rushing through the story too quickly, though. To really understand my journey, you should know my family background and the people who shaped the lives of my mother and me.

My maternal grandmother was named Maria; *Babcia,* as we called her. She was born in Ropczyce, Poland, in 1889. To be more specific, she was born in Granice, a small rural suburb on the outskirts of town about a mile from the center of incorporated Ropczyce. Her mother died when she was nine years old, and she was raised by an abusive stepmother who cultivated a cold insensitivity in Babcia's personality; a mark Babcia carried throughout her life.

At the time of Babcia's birth, Ropczyce functioned as part of the former Austro-Hungarian region of Galicia and was prominently inhabited by Polish Catholics and Jews. During those years, the common classification of Ropczyce was that of a *shtetl,* a very small town with a large population of pious orthodox Jews.[1] Poland, despite being surrounded by the numerous social, political, and religious conflicts of other countries, had become known for its tolerance toward Jews, and from there developed one of the world's largest and most vibrant Jewish communities.[2]

Ropczyce changed hands many times before and during Babcia's early life. During Babcia's early years, Galicia was the rope in a complex tug-of-war among Germany, Austria-Hungary, and Russia, concerning which country would control the political and economic climate. Under such inconsistent and unstable conditions, prosperity bypassed the entire area. Almost nobody had a job. Those who were employed counted themselves in an exclusive class of people.

Ropczyce, however, having a history as a Polish "royal city," maintained administrative status as county seat and therefore sustained a small assembly of well-kept government buildings in the city center. The buildings were a mere façade for the poverty and hardship most families in the area experienced.

To put things in relative terms, the average life expectancy in Galicia around the nineteenth century was about twenty-seven years for men, and twenty-eight and a half years for women of the region, compared to thirty-nine and forty-one in France, and forty and forty-two in England. The quality of life was also much lower. The yearly consumption of meat did not exceed ten kilograms per capita, compared to twenty-four kilograms in Hungary, and thirty-three in Germany, mostly because of a much lower average income. On an informal level, the poverty was conveyed in a Polish nickname bestowed upon the kingdom of Galicia and Lodomeria, modern-day Ukraine. *Golicja i Głodomeria* translated loosely to "Naked and Hunger Land."[3]

To make matters worse, in 1913, a famine broke out and spread throughout Poland, the Ukraine, Austria-Hungary, and parts of Russia. The famine gained international attention when the *New York Times* reported on February 13, "The suffering is so (widespread) that the communal authorities are distributing bread and potatoes to the populace. Municipal funds for this purpose have become exhausted, however...." Considering the area's fragile state during that time, government leaders in the region ultimately dismissed the idea of investment into Galicia as "throwing money down a hole." The suffering continued.

In general, the Austro-Hungarian government used the region mostly as a reservoir of cheap labor and recruits for the army, as well as a buffer zone against Russia. It was not until the early 1900s that the development of heavy industry blossomed. Even then, it was mostly connected to war production. The biggest state investments in the region were the railways and the fortresses in larger cities, such as Krakow.

With few opportunities for sustaining an existence beyond survival, a mass emigration of impoverished Galician villagers got underway in the 1880s and continued into Babcia's formative years. The emigration started as a seasonal excursion to imperial Germany, which was newly unified and economically dynamic. When villagers returned from Germany to their homeland with stories that a better life could, in fact, be found, more and more of the population garnered the courage to pack up and go. The population shift soon evolved into a transatlantic one, with large-scale emigration to the United States and other countries in the western hemisphere.[3]

With so many emigrants departing for the United States during that period, Babcia heard countless stories about the opportunities America offered. Most people had jobs; they ate well and led a more tolerable life. These stories drove Babcia, at twenty-one, with her brother's help, to board a transatlantic ship bound for America.

On her arrival, Babcia settled in a Polish community in north central Pennsylvania, where she quickly found work cleaning homes. She also found a husband. She married Jan, a coal miner. *Dziadzio*, as his grandchildren called him, was born in Lezansk, Poland, a *shtetl* about fifty miles northeast of Ropczyce. He had come to the U.S. in search of work, like so many others.

Their marriage was tumultuous. Babcia's belligerent and harsh disposition dangled over the household, waiting for a spark to ignite an argument. Dziadzio drank. His drinking lit the fuse for some of their most colorful verbal disputes. When they fought, Babcia dug in her heels and settled in for the long haul. She was what I call an "endurance arguer." Quite often, she simply wore him down. One way or another, though, their arguments came to a conclusion. Sometimes only one of them was left standing. If neither one gave in, or if Dziadzio's patience wore thin, he lashed out with the back of his hand. Despite the shaky foundation of their relationship, in keeping with their strong Catholic beliefs, they began a large family.

My mother, christened Maria Regina, was the third child in what began as a family of five children (one of whom died soon after birth). She was born in Williamsport, Pennsylvania, on March 12, 1916. Her earliest childhood memories were that of a fairly normal, but poor, young girl. She liked school. She was vivacious, fun loving, and gregarious.

Neither Dziadzio nor Babcia particularly enjoyed life in the United States, and the family never completely settled in to the faster-paced American lifestyle. Furthermore, their love for each other was deteriorating. Their lifestyle drew a sharp contrast to the American way of life that Babcia imagined. The fortune they hoped to amass in America fell far short of their expectations, so their dream of making enough money to move back to Poland and retire wealthy slowly faded with each passing day. They moved, periodically, to search for opportunities in a setting more like the home they knew back in Poland. After a few years in Pennsylvania, when prospects for employment dried up, the family moved again. Niagara Falls seemed like the next best bet. It wasn't too far a trip. It was also one of the few U.S. cities about which they knew something. They had heard about the famous falls and that they might have a better chance of getting a job there, so off they went.

While in the States, Babcia and the children went back and forth to Poland three times, leaving Dziadzio behind each time. They agreed he should stay behind to earn more, so the family could move back to Poland sooner. At the announcement of each trip, the household buzzed with excitement. Babcia packed, and the older children danced around at the prospect of riding the train and boarding the ship for the long journey. For Babcia and Dziadzio, it was a détente from the constant fighting between them. Mama, on the other hand, always had mixed feelings about leaving her *tatus* (Polish for father) for such long periods. They were close. Their relationship plainly contrasted Mama's fiery rapport with her mother.

The trip to Poland cost a small fortune. I often wondered how such a poor family could afford to travel to Europe so many times. The fact was, they couldn't afford it, but Babcia's steel will and irrational behavior usually overruled any logical reasoning. Dziadzio protested in vain.

The family stayed in Poland for several months on the first two trips. When the time came for them to return to the States, Babcia collected the children and their belongings. Babcia's close relatives, including a few uncles, aunts, and cousins, gathered to see them off. Some of the relatives gave Babcia fresh fruit and just-baked bread to bring along with them. Others offered their assurance of a safe trip. The men prepared the horse and hitched the wagon to it.

When everyone was packed and ready, Babcia and the four kids piled in for the bumpy ride, and Babcia's cousin drove them down the hill to the train station for a daylong journey to the harbor. As their second trip came to a close, the family arrived at the pier, handed over their tickets, and walked up the gangplank together. They were a large group by themselves, but their group was larger than even they knew. Babcia boarded the ship with two additional passengers in her womb, the result of a tryst with a man from a nearby village in Poland. She suspected a pregnancy. She never imagined twins. Still, while on board the ship, Babcia had more than enough time to concoct a credible story about the pregnancy without revealing the truth, and she did.

She arrived home with the children and settled back into her routine, never breathing a word of the affair. Babcia waited three months after returning home before breaking the news that she was expecting. Babcia was, by that time, four months pregnant and beginning to show. Dziadzio suspected nothing, although he did find it curious that she began to fill out so soon. Family and friends marveled at how quickly her midsection grew. "My goodness, this baby will be huge," remarked a friend.

As the time for the nearly full-term delivery grew near, Babcia ruminated over how to explain what would be considered an early birth. To her surprise and relief, Babcia delivered twins, her sixth and seventh children. She named them Jan and Janina. They appeared smaller in size than normal full-term babies, which allowed Babcia to easily explain their birth as "premature." Dziadzio again suspected nothing, nor did anyone else. The ever-growing family added greater financial challenges and even more stress to the household. The rift in their marriage grew wider daily.

As the months passed, Babcia romanticized about her homeland and the lover she left behind. Dziadzio's drinking increased, and their marriage continued to deteriorate. Despite the decline in their feelings toward each other, Babcia continued to perform her duties as a "good wife," and it wasn't long before she became pregnant with her eighth child, Stanley. Not one to let a pregnancy keep her down, Babcia announced her plans for a third trip to Poland. Dziadzio erupted, and they quarreled nonstop into the night. They argued over the trip. They argued over the cost. Dziadzio, at one point, insisted Mama stay in Niagara Falls with him. Babcia would not hear of it. Mama was twelve years old when she left the United States in 1928 on that journey to Poland. She didn't know it then, but she would never see her *tatus* again.

The best way to describe Mama's childhood in Poland is simple: she existed. Besides the work she was assigned, she led an uneventful

life. Even if she had more to do, time or money usually
ideas of distraction or amusement. Mama missed g
and because foreigners (she was an American) were noι ι
attend classes, her mother did not send her. Mama's contribution ι
the family income came first, so she and the rest of the children were
hired out to support the family. Her days in Granice were exhausting
and long. She milked and fed cows, cleaned stables, and served as a
common laborer for a local farmer. All the while, she wondered how
her father was faring back in the States.

As he had always done, Dziadzio continued to send money to
support the immediate family members while they were away. He
also sent money for the extended family. At some point, however,
word got out, and Dziadzio learned that some of his youngest
children, including the newborn Helena, were the product of Babcia's
infidelity. Whether the stark differences in appearance between the
first bed of children and the second triggered Dziadzio's suspicion,
I can only speculate. Soon thereafter, Dziadzio cut off all contact
with his family. They never heard from him again. We learned that
he developed diabetes and disregarded the symptoms as the disease
progressed. Doctors ultimately offered him the option of having his
legs amputated to save his life. Dziadzio refused and died in Niagara
Falls in 1944.

I never learned what became of the other man in Babcia's life.
Their relationship was apparently one of short-lived convenience
and self-satisfaction. In a Catholic family, such shortcomings were
not discussed except with a priest. I do know that he was not really
a part of their lives.

Work on the farm was grueling. Because nobody had money to
buy equipment, they did most of the work by hand. There was always
land to prepare, seeds to sow, and animals to tend. Each morning,
everyone rose before the sun came up and worked until dark, usually
in the same heavily mended, soiled, and sweaty clothes they wore the
day before. The dirt and dust settled on their moist skin, and with
the exception of their hands and face, was left to dry for a week or
so. When the workers weren't toiling in the fields, they cleaned the

home and stable, mended clothes, or repaired the house. Once in a while, a neighbor or relative visited after Mass on Sunday, the strictly observed day of rest.

Most of the local farmers grew wheat, potatoes, and cabbage on land that was over farmed. They had little in the way of seeds to support a successful crop yield, so families in the area usually went hungry. They ate what they could find whenever they could find it. Breakfast, lunch, or dinner—those concepts didn't exist. During the day, if they were hungry and saw a piece of bread, they ate it; otherwise, they simply went without.

As I learned in later years, we got used to hunger pangs. Depending on conditions, an evening meal usually consisted of something more substantial than bread. It may have included cabbage or potatoes. Summers added to the variety. Bountiful fruit trees and bushes dotted the landscape, and the fruit they produced was a welcome addition to their diet. They ate the fruit as it grew. They did not can the fruit, because they couldn't afford the jars.

Even after Babcia left Dziadzio, her oppressive personality did not soften. Because she had no husband, the responsibility fell on her to get food on the table and keep a roof over the heads of eight children. In her defense, Babcia was the mother and father of her large family, so she had to be strict. If anything, her approach to child rearing got even more strict and combative over time. She beat the children, usually with a broom, and often over insignificant things. Helena, the baby of the family, bore the brunt of Babcia's anger most often. Babcia beat Helena often over minor offenses. The children were generally obedient; if for no other reason than out of fear. Mama feared her mother. To varying degrees, so did the others.

Some parents are strict with their children, but one can see the love in the way they look at each other, the way they hug, and even joke with each other. Babcia's children never experienced that sort of attention. Taught by example, they showed little affection to their mother or to each other. Eventually an unspoken division developed between Dziadzio's children and those born later. That rift grew as the children grew, with some of the older siblings behaving coldly toward the younger ones, over time. In such a depressed environment, with no prospects for improvement, the hope for anything to brighten the tone in the household anytime soon was unlikely.

One exception was the love Mama held for her little sister Helena. Although sisters, Mama coddled and pampered Helena. She treated Helena as her own little girl. Mama fed her, held her, and hugged her. They went for long walks together along the dirt road outside their house on Sundays after church. They sang songs and talked about things little girls like to talk about. Along the way, they picked flowers and berries. At home, Mama loved to brush Helena's hair. She worked out the knots and brushed over and over until Helena's fine blond hair turned smooth and silky.

CHAPTER 2
HAPPILY MARRIED

In 1933, Babcia arranged the marriage of Mama to Wojtek Ziobro, my future father. Wojtek lived across the street with his parents, two houses from Babcia. After studying Wojtek's behavior and manner for some months, Babcia approached him with the prospect of marrying her daughter. Mama was seventeen. He was thirty-three. They were married in a Catholic ceremony in Ropczyce on June 5. The wedding presented a rare opportunity for all the family members to break from their mundane and dreary lives to celebrate something. Money didn't seem to matter. Food was plentiful. Everyone washed the dirt from their bodies and dressed in their Sunday best.

To put such an event into perspective, consider that the practice washing off happened infrequently. They had no running water, so the process of washing oneself involved a bucket carried from the well. They heated the water over the cinder stove until, after five or ten minutes, bubbles floated to the top and steam rose from the pot. One at a time, they dipped a rag into the warm water and rubbed the dirt off their skin. In a single-room house, they performed the process in the most modest way possible, despite often being surrounded by six or eight other members of the family; each of them eagerly waiting a turn. It was primitive, but they did the best they could with what they had. Still, nobody ever made much of such things. It's just the way life was.

The ceremony was a typical Polish wedding. Family and friends gathered at the Transfiguration of Jesus Catholic Church in Ropczyce to support my future mother and father as they exchanged their vows in front of the presiding priest. While everyone gathered into the church and the excitement of the moment built, Babcia noticed Helena was missing.

In great haste, before heading off to the church, Helena had dressed quickly and was headed out the door with the rest of the family, when some of the neighborhood children pulled her aside.

"I can't play right now. I'm going to church. My sister is getting married," she said.

"Aw, come on, Helena. Just play for a little while," they cajoled.

"No, I really don't have time. My family has already gone ahead, and I need to catch up to them."

"Helena, the church is right down the road. Play for a little while, and you'll have plenty of time to run to church. We'll even go with you."

Helena agreed, and the children darted off with Helena in the middle of the pack. They scampered past the pile of cow manure with just enough time for the older boy, running alongside Helena, to extend his leg directly into Helena's path. One of the other galloping children helped Helena to the ground with a passing shove. Helena's knees buckled, and she fell sideways. With arms outstretched, Helena landed directly in the manure pile.

As Helena lifted herself off the ground, in a split second of disbelief, everyone including Helena, stared at her once-sparkling white dress covered in compost. The other children quickly scattered and left Helena to deal with her dilemma by herself. She didn't have a clean change of clothes, and she was too embarrassed to walk to church to explain what had happened. Instead, she sat at the entrance to her house, sobbing.

Back at the church, family and friends gathered to pose for the wedding picture. When Helena couldn't be found inside the church, Babcia called a few of the children together and searched all around the church grounds for Helena, all the while calling her name. They retraced their steps back home to find Helena sitting outside the house, wearing her Sunday dress, and in tears.

As her mother and brother looked closer, they saw Helena's snow white dress covered in manure. They stepped closer and were greeted by the unmistakable stifling smell. Babcia erupted, "Helena, where have you been, and what have you done to your dress?"

They quickly helped her to remove her dress and get her cleaned up. Her regular clothes were badly soiled from the prior day's work. With no change of clothes, they wrapped Helena in blankets and hurried back to the wedding, leaving Helena in the house, by herself.

My father-to-be, Tatus to me, baptized Adalbertus Wojciech, was born July 29, 1900, in Brzyzna Poland, another rural village on Ropczyce's outer bounds. Wojteck, as he was better known, was one of four children. He had two brothers and a sister. His father, Wojciech married Katarzyna Gawlik (nicknamed Kasia) in the 1800s.

Tatus fought in World War I as a foot soldier. He served his country honorably, but brought back nagging memories of the war in the form of life-altering physical ailments. He returned home with a kidney infection. Doctors suspected he contracted the affliction from spending extended periods in foxholes. He rarely complained, but his increasing discomfort drew the attention of close family and friends. He frequented the local doctor, but the limited medical experience of that time and place proved ineffective in resolving the infection, so he lived with the pain. For his trouble, the government paid him the standard monthly pension of a disabled veteran.

After my parents' wedding, Mama's modesty left her too embarrassed to accept the responsibilities of marriage. She could not bring herself to move in with her new spouse. The beginning weeks of their marriage played out like a courtship. Mama stayed with Babcia for the first few months of their marriage, and Tatus patiently waited for his wife to adjust. Mama visited her husband, occasionally overnight, to get used to the concept of marriage.

Eventually Mama moved in with Tatus and his parents. They lived in a stable converted into a house, a one-room home with a single window and a dirt floor. The effects of the elements had taken their toll on the house exterior; turning what remained of the white paint to a curdled cream color. Weathered wood is a phrase that best describes the style and color of the exterior. The sun and wind peeled away most of the paint by the time Mama and Tatus moved in. Still, they were happy together, so little else really mattered.

Mama and Tatus had a good marriage. Their personalities blended perfectly, and they treasured each other. Tatus's calm and mild-mannered demeanor complemented Mama's outgoing and vivacious nature. They practiced their Catholic faith with the utmost devotion and sincerity; attending Mass often, especially the first Friday of the month, a common ritual for Roman Catholics at that time. Mama recalls only a single disagreement between them. Tatus loved Mama's long, flowing, light brown hair. Mama wanted to cut it. It got in the way of her work in the fields. Mama sometimes threatened to cut it, and they quibbled over it from time to time, but she didn't have the heart to make good on her threat.

Tatus spent his days in a dimly lit part of their house, making and repairing shoes for the neighborhood families. Electricity had not yet made its way to rural Granice, so the early morning sun provided the best light. In the evening, he strained his eyes using the muted flame of a candlestick to brighten an otherwise dark room. Seldom did he have the opportunity to make a brand-new pair of shoes. Few could afford them. People brought him their boots with badly torn soles. They brought deeply worn shoes that had been handed down from child to child. Some of the shoes had seen his handiwork multiple times over the years. His tools were simple and few. They were hand tools he purchased used. Without the sophisticated equipment of a modern shop, making or mending each pair of shoes often took days, sometimes weeks to complete.

Despite limited means, he was a craftsman, a perfectionist. He approached every pair of shoes as a work of art. Mama recalls his laboring in a methodical way for hours at a time. He never appeared frustrated or impatient. He found his work to be satisfying. Satisfying, but not particularly profitable. The limited supply of money in the neighborhood generated inventive methods of payment. Sometimes Tatus received eggs, chickens, vegetables, or whatever items of value his customers could offer. Other times, payment came as a promise for such things, when available.

When he wasn't making shoes, he spent his time outside in his yard. In the winter, pushing the fallen snow to one side or another ranked high on the small list of things to do, and he did plenty of that. A typical Polish snowfall in the deep winter measured about six inches to a foot. More than one of those in a week slowed activity in the neighborhood to a near stop. Snowplows didn't exist anywhere in the area. Residents piled the snow high along the walkways using makeshift shovels that had three parts: a board to capture the snow, a sturdy tree branch to use as the handle, and some sort of fastener to hold the two together.

Tatus treated Mama like a queen. He made her numerous pairs of shoes. He also let her buy material to make her own clothes. Mama, being from a poor family, thought she was in paradise. By comparison to her former way of life, she was. Still, Mama worked hard, as well. The family had apple, pear, and cherry trees and a large strawberry patch on the single-acre plot of land we called *Ziobrowka* (Job-roof-ka), named after the family. Mama farmed the land daily, in addition to the usual household chores. Most of their work had to be done during the day, because candle oil for the lantern was not always available.

One day Mama walked from their rural Granice home, down the hill, and into the center of Ropczyce. She spent the day wandering around the shops and stores, enjoying the mild hustle and bustle that could not be found in suburban Granice. She marveled at the dresses she could never afford and the scarves she would love to wear to church. She also peeked into the shoe store with a critical eye. *"Sure, the styles are more current here, but the quality can't match what my Wojteck can make,"* she confirmed to herself. She stopped into the mercantile to buy some salt, sugar, and flour. With her arms full, she paid the attendant at the counter. She headed toward the door, and her eye caught a glimpse of a crisp, neatly folded swatch of material at the far end of the store. One fold of the cloth had unraveled and draped itself over the edge of the merchandise table. The sunlight from the adjacent window bounced off the fabric, creating a subtle glow that was too hard to resist. Even though Mama and Tatus didn't have enough money to spend on anything beyond the essentials, she walked over to the table and stood there, imagining herself tailoring the material into a magnificent dress.

She carefully placed her bag of groceries on the floor and picked up the material from the basket in which it was displayed. *"Perfect color,"* she mused. A pale blue. She tugged at the cloth to gauge its sturdiness. It would certainly last for many years. *"With some of the remnants I have at home, I could embroider a white fringe around the hem. It would look elegant,"* she thought. With a nod of satisfaction, she picked up the material and her bag of groceries and headed back to the counter to add to her purchase. She left the store and made her way back home in time to see the sun drop out out view, beyond the tree line.

When she approached the house, she felt an increasing sense of guilt for what she had bought. She worried Tatus would be angry at her. After coming into the house, she sheepishly walked over to her husband at his work table to confess her impulsive purchase. She proceeded to make her case, her justification for what might be considered a frivolous expense. Tatus saw the look of remorse on her face and interrupted. "Maria, we are partners," he said. "If you make a decision, it is as though I made the decision with you. I am not at all upset. Show me the material. I can't wait to see how it looks on you."

One day, Mama walked down the road to visit her mother and siblings back at the old house. For her sister Helena, it was always a special occasion when Mama came over. Even though they lived close by and saw each other often, each visit brought with it an air of excitement, as if they hadn't seen each other in weeks. When Helena caught sight of Mama, she ran toward her. Mama's greeting seemed less energetic than usual, offering a warm, but reserved hug.

Bouncing up and down, Helena begged Mama to carry her. Mama uncharacteristically declined.

The family proceeded into the house and gathered around the table. Helena raced to Mama and patiently waited to be hoisted into Mama's lap. Again, Mama politely declined. Puzzled, Helena stood close by until Mama cautiously pulled a calmer Helena onto her lap.

Each person settled into their usual spot and the discussion commenced. The topics of the day were no different than any other: work, the cost of sugar and flour and other staple food items, the state of the world, the family's health, and what the neighbors were doing. After a few hours, it was time to head home. Mama said her good-byes and started down the dirt road back to her house. Helena stood in front of the window, and watched her sister with a concerned look. Babcia closed the door and headed back into the house. Helena remarked, "Maria must be very sick. When I sat on her lap, I noticed her stomach has gotten very fat since the last time we saw her."

Babcia said, "It's because she ate too much *kapusta*."

Later, Helena learned that Mama was, in fact, not fat, but pregnant.

Another month passed, and at eighteen, Mama gave birth to me, Cecylia Teresa, on June 1, 1934, a few months before Adolf Hitler became *führer* of Germany. A midwife brought me into the world in my father's old house. The delivery was typical: boiling water to sanitize things. Blankets, towels, and lots of anxious waiting. Following the delivery, Mama stayed off her feet for only a few days, before she went back to work.

As a baby, although various people in the family cared for me, I spent most days with Babcia. When Aunt Helena got older, if she wasn't working for the local farmer, she stayed around my father's house to play with me and keep me occupied. One day Mama returned from work to find that Aunt Helena had taught me to walk. She and I did lots of things together while Mama was at work. She took me to church and to pick flowers. We did many of the same things that Mama did with Aunt Helena when they were younger.

We'd walk along the road picking red poppies and swine's cress, a long, bright yellow flower that prominently grew along the roads and in the fields of our village. Ornamental trees or shrubbery had no place in Granice. Anything planted had to produce a yield of some sort to support the local residents. The fruit trees and bushes growing in family gardens, on small farms, and along the roads in Granice served that purpose well. Moreover, with the vibrant colors of the flowers and trees that blossomed in the early summer, our village resembled a painter's palette of pastels and brilliant shades of pink, yellow, green, and blue.

Although Tatus's yard was well maintained and he provided food and shelter for the family, the disappointment that he couldn't provide a better life for his wife and young child troubled him. He had big dreams. He promised my mother to take us to America, some day. With my father's income from his shoe business, along with his military pension, we were still poor, but we were never short of food. I don't recall ever being hungry during those times. Nonetheless, Tatus was frugal with his resources.

Mama once packed a basket of food to bring to Babcia and her family. She filled it with freshly baked bread, *kapusta* (a cabbage-based dish with seasonings), cabbage-filled pierogi, and cheese-filled *naleshniki* (thin pancakes). She packed some milk and covered the warm food with a white cotton napkin. She closed up the basket and headed out the door and across the dirt road to her mother's house. When she returned, Tatus, who watched her bake and cook the entire afternoon, inquired, "Where's all that food you made?" When she told him she had taken it over to her mother's house, his displeasure was apparent. "I don't mind that you help your family once in a while," he said with a twinkle in his eye, "as long as we don't starve in the process."

Tatus and his mother-in-law enjoyed a civil and reasonably friendly relationship; at least as friendly as one could be with her. Although he was unhappy with Mama for helping out her family so much, his discontent wasn't particularly directed at Babcia. He simply made the point that we needed to take care of ourselves before we get too charitable.

When she wasn't working, Babcia visited friends and relatives in the neighborhood. She enjoyed being in the company of others and enjoyed idle conversation. She never kept her opinion to herself, and she loved to debate a point; whether she had a valid argument or not. She was gone so often that when I got older I sometimes asked her, "Where are you going, Babcia?" To which she always responded, "I'm going to Honolulu." To me, Honolulu sounded like a fairy tale place. I giggled at the sound of the name.

CHAPTER 3
HOLY MARY, MOTHER OF GOD

Tatus was determined to provide a better life for his family. Despite the lethargy caused by his illness, he began to build a new home for us. Each morning he headed out into the fields, through the forest and along the pathways, in search of materials he could use to build our new home. He left for hours at a time, gathering wood to use for lumber, stones for the foundation, and thatch for the roof. The stones he needed were awkwardly heavy and difficult to lift.

His approach for locating materials was as methodical as his approach to all things. From our house, he walked the common ground of our neighborhood in circles, a few acres at a time. In one hand he carried a solid tree branch, about three inches thick and four feet long; which he used as a fulcrum for leverage. It doubled as a walking stick. He whittled one end to a chisel point, making it easier to drive into the soil and dislodge an embedded stone. He carried a rope over his shoulder and a burlap bag under his arm. Across his back hung a borrowed shovel tied to a leather strap he held in his other hand.

He kept a slow pace. Except for a self-imposed deadline to finish before the sun went down, rushing seldom served a purpose. When he found a stone, he rolled it onto the burlap bag and pulled it home. With any luck, he could roll the stone at least part of the way. Otherwise, he had to dig the stone up and drive the tree branch underneath it to roll it out of the ground and onto the burlap bag. Depending on the size of the stone and the distance from the house, it could take him half the day to get a single stone home. The work was backbreaking for a healthy man. For a man in Tatus's condition, it was debilitating. He often came home with barely enough energy to eat. Sometimes he toweled off his sweaty, aching body. Other times he merely dragged himself to his straw mattress for the night; preparing for another day of the same.

As a diversion from rolling and dragging stones, he set aside wood he found along the way. Hunting for lumber to frame the house had its own set of challenges. We lived near a forest owned by a local neighbor. The man who owned the land allowed us to collect the trees lying on the ground. Unfortunately, the forest was usually clean of fallen trees. Tatus still managed to accumulate a substantial pile of wood outside the old house.

Autumn arrived, and with it came cooler air and the vibrant foliage that covered Ropczyce's rolling hills. By late October, Tatus gathered enough materials to begin assembling the frame of our new home. He contently surveyed his resources, standing in the yard with his hands on his hips as he often did. He looked up at the sky, evaluating the low, dense clouds. Winter was coming. Sunset came earlier each day, and before long, the first snow of the season blanketed the frozen ground. Tatus postponed building until spring.

The snow cleared in April. Mama hoped the long rest through the winter would help Tatus recover. It did not. Mama blamed the worsening of his prolonged sickness on the stones he carried from the field, and she urged him to put the project on hold until he regained his strength. He never considered it. Tatus broke ground on wet, slushy soil, amid stifling back pain. The sullen expression on his face told the story of a man who, despite the best intentions for completing his new home, faced an uphill struggle. His health deteriorated further. He managed to frame four walls, although eventually he had no choice but to lay down his hammer. Over time his condition worsened and as the days went by, he found himself lying in bed writhing in pain. He anguished over the thought that the hours of laborious effort to build his house were wasted. A cure for his kidney ailment did not exist, so the family members did the only thing they knew to do. They prayed for his recovery.

The most prominent memory I have of Tatus is one from those tormented days. I was barely three years old. We were both outside on that afternoon. I played in the yard. The warmth of the sun against the light breeze was a perfect match for the new green grass at the beginning of summer. A pure blue sky cast a blanket of good spirits over everyone. Everyone except Tatus. He lay on a feather comforter Mama placed on the most level ground she could find. He lay there trying to get comfortable, but clearly not succeeding. I wondered how I could ease his pain so he could enjoy the marvelous day with the rest of us. Looking toward his garden, I spotted his prized strawberries. In my three-year-old mind, the fact that they were perfectly green had no bearing on my decision. With great haste, I dropped what I was doing and scurried over to the garden. As fast as my little fingers could pick, I gathered the berries into my dress, carefully folding the hem of my apron toward me to ensure that none of the strawberries slipped out. Once I had picked every last one, I bobbled back to where he lay. "Tatus, this will make you feel so much better!"

He slowly turned his head toward me. His eyes moved methodically down toward the apron of my dress. In a solemn tone, he said, "Do you see that stick over there?"

"Yes, Tatus."

"Bring it over here to me."

Puzzled, I obediently ran over and retrieved the stick. The next thing I knew, I was face down over his knees. When it was over, I had learned the difference between ripe and unripe. I ran to my mother, who did her best to console me; explaining the lesson in terms I could more easily grasp. I wish I had better memories of my father.

After that, Tatus spent most of his days lying in bed, fidgeting and moaning in pain. One afternoon, while Mama was on her way back to work in the fields, she brought me to Tatus to take a nap with him in his bed. She thought it might be comforting for him to have his daughter nearby. I liked the idea of simply being close to him; something that rarely happened. He wore a flannel shirt. A bed sheet covered his body. Mama helped me into the bed, and I curled up beside him. I don't know how long I lay there, but I never got a wink of sleep. His pain was so intense that he kicked and writhed enough to keep me awake the whole time. I eventually crawled out of bed and ran outside to Mama. She understood and sent me off to play.

Granice was a charming village during those days, picturesque from every angle and rich in soil. Unfortunately, that is all that was rich. Granice was a farm community, a suburb of Ropczyce. Dreadfully poor people worked the land, mostly by hand. Horses were scarce, and equipment even more so.

As kids, we had no toys, so we played games with each other, made mud pies, or played with the sticks we found on the ground. Cold and snowy winters reduced our chances to play due to our lack of warm clothes. The summer, however, opened a treasure chest of fun things to do. We'd wade barefoot in the stream at the bottom of the hill, and skip stones. Sometimes we headed off into the forest to pick flowers, gather berries, or simply to walk.

One summer day, Aunt Julia, Mama's younger sister, took me blueberry picking. We headed into the forest and meandered down the trail with a watchful eye, in the hunt for any sign of the deep, dark contrast of a blueberry against an otherwise green landscape. It was a matter of pride for every family member to contribute to the family's well-being in whatever way they could. Of course as a young child, my contribution was often quite small.

We made our way deep into the woods. The fir trees hovering over us grew increasingly dense while the rays of sunlight struggled to burn through the branches above. We stepped across a large rock sitting in the middle of the trail and climbed over the trunk of a fallen tree into a clearing, where the tree branches gave way to a few extra rays of sunlight. Through the breeze-blown branches, the sunlight danced on the edge of a huge blueberry patch, seemingly hinting for us to "pick here." The blueberries were perfectly ripe, plump, and plentiful. A deep blue and purple color covered the forest floor for at least ten or twenty paces, over a small hill and off into the near distance. Our excitement at the sight fueled an overwhelming desire to drop to our knees. We picked as fast as we could, as though if we didn't, the berries might disappear before our eyes.

When our buckets were full we returned to the house, and I proudly displayed my small but overflowing pail of berries to Babcia, sitting at the table with a friend who was visiting. Babcia said, "Aren't you going to treat my friend to some of your berries?"

Hmmm. I wasn't so sure. After all, Mama had not yet seen the fruits of my labor. I reluctantly approached her friend. Hoping she would take a polite berry or two, I inched the pail toward her. In an instant, she grabbed my whole bucket and ate every last blueberry, all by herself! All that hard work, and nothing to show for it. "Nasty old woman," I murmured under my breath.

The neighborhood in Granice was made up primarily of elderly people, but a few families had young children about my age, including my father's nephew. We all played together. I suppose we were not really close friends, because I can't recall any of the other kids' names. We played hide and seek, tag, and the usual childhood games. When I think back to how destitute the area was, it's curious that as children, we never concerned ourselves with that fact or dwelt on it. Sure, we were hungry at times, but wasn't everyone? We heard stories about how things were so much better in the United States, but only in our dreams did we entertain such thoughts.

When I wasn't playing with the neighborhood kids, I spent a great deal of time in our cherry tree, eating cherries and thinking about who I might marry. I wondered how I might look when I grew up. And yes, what it would be like to live in America. I probably thought about going to America more than the other kids, because I knew my mother was born there, and some of my relatives had been there. Most likely I thought about America because Mama never gave up the dream of going back, and she talked about it regularly.

I knew about America before I knew how to spell and write in Polish. Mama taught me "apples, peaches, pumpkin pie" in English. One thing I did not know is that I was an American from birth, something I learned only after we came to America. "For any American who went abroad and had a child, the U.S. government classified that child as an American citizen." At that time, few people knew the law existed. Fewer were able to take advantage of it, because the United States repealed the law in 1941.

That cherry tree held special meaning to me. It was the only tree Tatus allowed me to climb because it was the only established tree on the property. The cherries were always super sweet, pinkish, always plump and bright in color, perfectly formed. Tatus planted some red cherry trees in the back yard, but he told me they were too young and fragile to climb, so I didn't.

Every day I ran to my tree, grabbed the same branch closest to me, and hoisted myself up. I worked my way to the top of the tree, placing each foot in the same spot every time, as though the branches were marked for every step of the way. Sometimes I tried to get out on the smaller branches, purely for the challenge of it. Considering the number of times I lost my footing, it's amazing I never came crashing to the ground.

When I reached the top, inches above the roofline, I looked around imagining that everything in sight were part of my kingdom. I saw the straw roofs of the surrounding houses and the trees lining the dirt road. In the distance I saw the town of Ropczyce. I saw the school I would briefly attend. I saw our church. Sometimes in the late afternoon I stared at the sun as it fell from view, wondering how far it was to the horizon and how long it would take to get there. I promised myself, "When I grow up, I will find out what's out there."

Also, from high in my perch, I wondered what I would be when I grew up. I knew my Tatus had big dreams for me. He planned to send me to school, all the way to the University of Krakow. Whatever the future held for me, I would make sure Tatus was proud of me.

Say what you want about Babcia, and many people did; nonetheless, she did have a strong sense of responsibility for what was right, even though many times, her opinion of "what was right" was way off the mark. When Tatus's life neared its end, Babcia took him into her house to help my mother care for him. In his final days, his life was a painful experience for everyone. In Tatus's weakened and helpless condition, Babcia and Mama literally had to drag him outside and hold him up so he could go to the bathroom on top of the manure pile. The experience whittled my father's sense of pride down to nothing. Certainly Babcia and Mama found the practice to be physically and emotionally tiring, but it needed to be done, so they did it.

On June 27, 1937, Tatus died at thirty-seven years old. I was three years and twenty-six days old. When he died, Babcia talked Mama into moving in with her. Mama brought a cow and a calf to Babcia's house. The calf was unfortunately not with us for long. The priest insisted he could not bury Tatus until he received money for the funeral, so Mama sold the calf and gave the money to the priest. *"How strange for a priest to be so concerned about money,"* I thought. They say that money makes the world go around—even when doing "the Lord's work," I suppose.

Tatus's body was laid out in Babcia's home. During those days, we prayed and cried. For two days, we slept in the attic on straw to make room for his casket and provide a sitting area for those who came by to pay their respects. It was kind of eerie knowing Tatus's body lay below us, on the ground floor. Listening to the adults talk about his ghost was even more eerie.

They didn't embalm people in those days. The procedure was quite expensive. Instead they covered his face with a cloth to hide the effects of the summer heat. At his wake, about twenty or so people joined us in the room to mourn. The mood was somber. Most of the women cried. Mama sobbed. At times, her body convulsed. It made me cry to see her so overwhelmed.

I wanted to see my Tatus, so I made my way over to Aunt Genevieve, Mama's sister. I raised my hands above my head, motioning for her to lift me up.

"What is it, Celinka?" she said as she hoisted me up. Huffing and puffing, she wrapped her arm around my back, lifted me up, and balanced me on her hip.

"I want to see Tatus, but I can't see over the edge of the box they put him in," I said in a helpless tone.

"You've grown so big, Celinka, I can barely hold you anymore. Let me put you down for a minute." She put me back down on the floor and scooched down to my eye level. With comforting eyes and a kind smile she said, "I'll take you over to see your tatus." Holding hands, we walked past the relatives standing nearby and the few hand-picked flowers that served to brighten the solemn mood. Aunt Genevieve stood behind me and jostled me right up to the front of the casket, where my nose was inches from the simple pine box. I looked up, but could merely see a thin, white blanket that covered my father's body. Aunt Genevieve fitted her hands under my armpits. I heard her struggling behind me. My feet finally left the ground. My neck stretched, and my eyes strained to see over the coffin's edge, as my range of sight widened slower than my patience allowed.

I had grown rather big by that time, and it was clear by the way I swayed back and forth in her outstretched arms that Aunt Genevieve couldn't hold me much longer. When she tried to pull away the cloth covering my father's face, Aunt Genevieve lost her grip on me and almost dumped me into the coffin with him. I began to fall, but managed to catch a glimpse beneath the cloth. What I saw terrified me. Pimples, red welts, and bruises covered the grey stoic face that was once my father. Aunt Genevieve regained her grip on me before I fell any farther and put me back on solid ground. I never got over the horror I had experienced. It haunted me the rest of my life.

After seeing my father in a coffin, I felt a great sense of loss. Two days later, the family buried him, and Mama was a widow at twenty-one. Aunt Genevieve held me in her arms at the cemetery, and I watched some of the men lower the yellow pine casket into a deep, dark hole. The relatives from each side of the family attended, about ten to fifteen people. Mama cried, "Wojtus! Wojtus! Why did you leave me?" On her knees she pleaded with him to come back to her. They lowered the body into the earth, and she got down on her hands, following the casket as it made its way into the grave. The farther they lowered it, the closer Mama inched toward it, screaming and sobbing all the while. At one point, someone had to hold Mama back. It seemed as though she wanted to follow Tatus into the ground.

After the funeral, we walked solemnly back to the house. Nobody said a word. With Tatus gone, Mama's life changed in a matter of days. She sold the shoemaking equipment, piece by piece, and the partially finished home. For a long time, she went about her work, both in the house and out in the field, showing little emotion. She certainly showed little love or affection toward me.

I continued to mourn the loss of my father. I had bad dreams after he died, dreams undoubtedly brought on by an overwhelming belief in ghosts by those around me. Everyone feared the dead. Adults routinely spoke of the dead coming back to life. Some even claimed to have seen dead people. My Babcia, for example, said she saw my father's spirit several times. She saw people climbing trees and ladders. Many old people reportedly felt the presence of their spouses after they died. The concept of ghosts always puzzled me. I never saw ghosts, but people I knew and respected for many years claimed to have seen them, sometimes frequently.

With Tatus gone, Mama understandably did not rush to remarry. That didn't stop the many suitors who were drawn to her. She was a good-looking woman who had no trouble attracting a husband on her own. Regardless, family members often tried to set her up with various friends and acquaintances. She politely declined every single one. Babcia also tried to introduce her to gentlemen she knew or had met. On one occasion, Mama got enraged. "Leave me alone," she said. "You married me off once! You won't do it again!"

Although Mama had agreed to move in with her mother, the relationship remained fragile. Babcia may have wanted her daughter to move in with her for a number of reasons. Sure, she felt obligated as a mother. She also thought they could all benefit from having an additional set of hands around the house. But more than anything, Babcia craved control. She probably perceived our moving in as an opportunity to regain control of her daughter. At that point in her life, however, Mama was not inclined to be forced under anyone's thumb, and she was prepared to stand her ground no matter who pressed her.

With the money she brought from America, Babcia was able to afford a decent house, by Granice standards. It had a wood floor and a straw roof. It was certainly a few steps up from our previous home. It was also the only house in the neighborhood with a floor made of more than the bare ground. The house had one large room which led to a stable for two cows. On the left was the entrance to the large room that held several beds and a closet. The walls were painted white. The outside of the house was also white.

On the right of the large room stood a large cinder wood stove. Two huge, at least four-foot-tall, holy pictures hung on a wall. One depicted the Sacred Heart of Jesus. The other was of Mary, the mother of Jesus, whose eyes followed me wherever I walked. One window separated the two large pictures, and another window was on the left. The stable was actually inside the house under the same roof, and on the outside of the house sat a manure pile. Being too poor to have an outhouse, we went to the bathroom there, as well, usually at night, when nobody was around. The house always smelled like manure.

Babcia had about three acres of land on which grew a number of fruit trees. The property was not as well kept as my father's had been, but it was fertile. Babcia and her children all worked the land. In exchange for food, Babcia also rented out her large room as a reception hall for the occasional neighborhood wedding. Babcia's wood floor added an air of class to the event that nobody else could afford to have in their own homes. It also made dancing much more enjoyable and certainly less dusty.

One day, a few months after Tatus's funeral, when Mama returned from the fields, she noticed a lump on the back of my head about the size of a grapefruit. It appeared barely above my neck. Strange that, despite its size, I didn't even feel it. Some said I got the affliction from sleeping in the drafty attic. Nobody had ever seen anything like it, but it seemed that someone always came up with a reason for why things happened. Whether the reason made sense or not, having a reason was more comforting than not having one.

A trip to the doctor was rare, but in this case Mama wanted professional advice. We left the house early the next morning and walked down the hill into the center of town. I had never been to see a doctor. I imagined it as similar to when the adults stood around me in Babcia's big room, talking about my condition as though I weren't even there. If that's what a visit to the doctor was like, I didn't much care for the idea.

"She has water on the back of her head. We need to operate immediately," the doctor told my mother.

"Operate?" Mama's eyes opened wide and her head jerked back. Can't we simply bleed the fluid out?" she pleaded with him. "Maybe hot compresses?"

"Operate." The word was so formal and technical. Worst of all, it required her to entrust the safety of her only child to a complete stranger.

"No," she decided. That was not going to happen. She left the doctor's office and hurried home.

She relayed the story to her mother, and Babcia gathered the family, who agreed the only alternative was to turn to God for help. Mama, Babcia, and the rest of the family prayed a novena to the Virgin Mary. Over and over, day after day, the family prayed. They prayed in the morning. They prayed out loud in the fields, and at night before bed. "Holy Mary, Mother of God, pray for us, sinners, now and at the hour of our death. Amen." So went the last lines of the "Hail Mary," part of the rosary they prayed over and over in a petition to the Blessed Virgin.

To someone who does not believe in God or the power of prayer, it's hard to comprehend the faith of a Polish Catholic family at that time. The fervor and devotion with which they prayed was truly remarkable. The unwavering confidence that their collective efforts would bring about a miracle was inspiring.

As an additional display of devotion and sacrifice, the family visited Czestochowa (Chen-sto-ho-va), a small city 150 miles west of Ropczyce, where a holy shrine to the Black Madonna stands. It is known to Poles and people throughout the world as a site of miracles. When the Hussites invaded Poland in 1430, they burned the church at Czestochowa to the ground. The only thing left standing among the ashes was the statue of the Blessed Madonna, whose only casualty was the smoke from the fire, which turned her face black.

On my family's return from Czestochowa, they continued their pilgrimage for nine more days at the local Matka Boska (Statue of the Blessed Virgin) in Ropczyce. Sure enough, one day while I played in the yard, the water broke. Someone wiped the water off my shoulders, and in time, the skin adhered to my head and healed without a trace. I never felt any pain. Truly a miracle! It later struck me that even after the family confirmed the affliction left no lasting effects, they said little about how or why I was healed. With all of that effort to pray for a miracle, nobody openly acknowledged it once their prayers were answered. They believed in the power of prayer and the result was proof of what they already knew.

CHAPTER 4
THE WAR

In late 1938, word was spreading that war was imminent. Mama wanted to return to America. Babcia insisted her son Walter, one of the oldest children, go first, because he could earn more money as a man and then bring everyone to America sooner than if one of the women went. Mama sold the second calf to pay for Uncle Walter's boat fare in 1938. When he came to the States, the Great Depression was well underway. It took a long time, but Uncle Walter managed to make ends meet taking menial jobs here and there.

About once a month, Uncle Walter sent a letter telling the family back home about living conditions, food, prospects for work, and the people he met. None of the information was particularly exciting or earthshaking. He was simply making his way, despite the hurdles of a language barrier, little knowledge of the culture, and no education or marketable skills. Eventually Uncle Walter moved to upstate New York where he found steady work in the Niagara Falls area. The letters, although less frequent, kept coming. The news, although not laced in silver or gold, was also improving. Each letter placed another log on the fire of hope that Mama held for returning to America.

During those days, Mama embarked on a daily routine of information gathering about the war. She circulated through the village, sharing with the locals Uncle Walter's news about what life was like in America. In exchange, she collected second- and third-hand information on pre-war events: who was fighting with whom, where they were thought to be bombing next, and if the fighting was expected to reach Ropczyce. Fear, anxiety, and a little edginess were always present in our house at that time, but never despair. As long as the sun was up, Mama was planning and gathering information.

Her nights were different. With her lively and fun-loving personality and the friends she made during the day, Mama quickly found her spot on the local social scene. Ropczyce was certainly not New York or Los Angeles; not even close. But during those times, Mama did her share of merrymaking. Every few nights, she hurried off to someone's house where the locals sang, danced, and told stories. Such diversions were probably quite therapeutic for a woman who had recently lost her husband. It didn't do our relationship any favors, though. I resented her for it. Each night while she fixed her hair, I pleaded with her to stay with me.

"Where are you going, Mama?"

"I'm going out."

"Out where?"

"To see some friends."

"What friends?"

"You know, Celina. The same friends as I saw the other night."

"If you just saw them the other night, why can't you stay home tonight with me instead?"

"Celina, stop asking the same questions all the time."

I followed her when she headed for the door. "Please, Mama! Don't leave. Stay here with me."

I don't recall ever being able to change her plans. The door closed in front of my Babcia and me, but I made sure Mama could hear me through the walls.

Babcia did her best to calm me. As hard a woman as she was, her demeanor softened in my company. Aside from her difficulties relating to her husband and children, my memories of our direct interactions are mostly pleasant. When we were together, her eyes seemed almost tender and her tone gentle, even playful. We developed a close relationship. I suppose it's not unusual for a parent to share a softer side to a grandchild. Having Babcia there fulfilled some of

my childhood needs for attention, which were not otherwise being
fulfilled. In some ways, I probably filled the gaps in her life, too.

As the days passed, talk of oceans filled with bombs and
mines scared Mama so much that her plan to leave Poland proved
impossible. She was not going to leave under those conditions, so we
stayed in Granice and awaited the war. Mama finally cut her long,
flowing, light brown hair that my tatus liked so much, but she kept
the braided locks and placed it in the closet to remind her of better
times.

Poland was in a depression, along with most of Europe and the
rest of the world. Jobs and resources to work the land dwindled
further. At the end of 1938, desperate to find work, Mama left for
Germany to work in a cafeteria for several months. That time away
from Mama seemed like years. It felt like a part of my body had been
taken from me. Although Babcia took good care of me, I longed for
my mother.

My father's pension and the milk from our cow kept a barely
sustaining amount of food on the table. The family neglected the
Ziobrowka land. Weeds and brush slowly infiltrated the grounds.
Regardless, my father's relatives often fought over who officially
owned the land. They argued with my mother that the land should
be returned to them because Tatus was no longer alive.

Meanwhile, negotiations over larger partitions of land were
well under way. On August 23, 1939, Germany and the Soviet
Union signed a public agreement of non-aggression; promising not
to go to war against each other. A secret condition of that pact gave
Estonia, Latvia, and Lithuania to Russia. Poland was to be split
between the two countries. This provision was granted by Germany
to ensure that Russia "looked the other way" if war "happened to
break out in Europe." Their pact assured Hitler that, in the event of
another war, the Germans would not have to fight on two fronts.
In retrospect, that agreement proved a well-calculated, preparatory
step directly into World War II. From that point, things around us
moved quickly.

Mama returned from Germany soon thereafter. When she arrived home, I felt complete again, but I kept those feelings to myself. She entered the door, and pulled a hand painted, delicately dressed doll from her bag. She bent over and with a tender smile, offered it to me. *"I won't let her off that easy,"* I thought. I grabbed the doll from her hand and tore it to pieces right in front of her. In defiance, I stood there staring directly into her eyes for a moment. Then, I turned and walked away.

Uncle John, a teenager at the time, told me in a calm, sarcastic tone, "Let's put that rag of a doll to good use, now that it's in pieces." The windows and doors, cooled by the outside air, dripped with condensation. "Why don't you go over and wash the windows and door with it, so we can see outside?" he laughed.

Even though I had torn the doll apart, I still felt attached to it in some strange way. It proved to me that regardless of how little time my mother spent with me, I still mattered to her. When winter came, I put its eyes on a snowman's head. I don't know where the doll ended up, but it held an important place in my memory over the years.

Almost a week passed and my anger subsided, but Mama's behavior never changed. She always had "somewhere else to go." Whether she was off to work or to socialize, she still had little time for me. Once or twice each week, I reminded Mama that I demanded her attention. I issued those demands with the delivery of one of my classic tantrums. I staged each tantrum to directly coincide with the time she spent getting ready to leave. What I never allowed Mama to see is that, following each of my performances and after she left the house, I typically slithered under my bed cover to hide the hurt that flowed from my eyes. To counteract the emotional wounds, I spent a fair amount of time that year plotting ways to express my frustration. I took her braided hair out of the closet, twirled it in the air, and told my Babcia, "Look! Look, Babcia, how Mama's head is jumping!" It wasn't long before those events proved trivial in comparison to what was in store for us.

On September 1, 1939, Adolph Hitler invaded Poland from the west. I was five years and three months old. It was a clear and sunny day, when someone ran to me in my father's garden and told me to hide under a tree. "The Germans are bombing Ropczyce!" he screamed.

I looked down the hill, and sure enough, I could see planes in the distance. Fire and smoke hovered over churches and schools. Our town was in flames.

"If the pilots don't see any people moving around, they'll pass over us," someone yelled.

We all huddled together under the trees and waited. We talked about what might become of us if German soldiers marched into Granice. We had heard stories of burned villages, rapes, and beatings. Babcia always said if the Germans came, she planned to hide in the hole under her house, where she kept perishables like milk, potatoes, and cabbage. Babcia also told us that during World War I, when Russian soldiers invaded Poland, they raped women and girls. As a common practice to prevent such a tragedy, when soldiers stormed into villages, young women and girls masked themselves with feces to avoid getting harmed. We prepared ourselves, mentally and emotionally.

We waited, and the bombs kept falling. I held the tree trunk tightly, thinking the tighter I held, the safer I'd be. From beneath the tree, I mimicked the adults, looking up through the leaves to the heavens to see if I could spot the planes flying past us. The first round of planes rushed past so quickly, they were mostly a blur, but I kept my eyes fixed on the sky. *"Can't someone save us?"* I thought. *"If only a plane could come down, scoop us up, and bring us to America,"* I dreamed. Dreams seldom came true in Ropczyce during those years.

The next round of planes came much nearer to the ground. The roar of the engines sounded so close that I thought the planes themselves would clip the treetops. The fighters swept past us one by one, each one taking my breath away while it roared past. I gritted my teeth, lowered my head, shut my eyes, and prepared for a bomb to land. I held close to the tree. My body convulsed with fright. As tightly as I clung to the tree and as much as my body shook, had there been any fruit on the trees, I probably could have shaken a few cherries loose, or so it felt.

More time passed, maybe an hour, and the bombing stopped. I released my grip of the tree trunk and noticed that the texture of its bark had pressed its image into my hands and face. We all went back to what we were doing, with one eye toward the sky. Everyone was clearly shaken, and our voices had a more serious tone. The end of the day came, and we saw no German soldiers ... at least not that day.

Poland was grossly unprepared for war. It was unexpectedly attacked by German air and ground forces from the west, while Russian planes and tanks moved in from the east. Many proud Polish soldiers fought bravely to protect their motherland with limited supplies, resisting their oppressors with a few planes, but mostly on horseback. Other Poles saw the futility in standing their ground and instead escaped to other countries to fight Hitler from more effective vantage points. Some went to England and Italy, and some even joined the French Underground.

After a few days, we walked to Ropczyce to assess the damage the Nazis inflicted on our schools and churches. I saw streets filled with German tanks, trucks, and soldiers. It was the first time I saw a motor vehicle. We arrived at what was once a quaint neighborhood with bright, pastel painted homes, some upscale, mixed in with government buildings. Aside from the horse-drawn carriages in the tree-lined streets, the quaint neighborhood I once knew was a war zone. Some of the roofs on the houses were missing. The smell of smoldering wood and smoke lingered. Soldiers filled the streets, at least two hundred. Some were giving orders. Screaming orders, was a more accurate description. We cautiously moved closer. It looked as though soldiers and townspeople were moving great numbers of things around, from one place to another, with little apparent progress or any particular purpose.

As we got closer, the purpose became clear. I saw the local Jewish townspeople assembled into small groups. To my horror, I watched while some were dragged from their homes and thrown into the street, five, six, seven at a time. Men, women, children. It didn't matter. I saw one man arguing with two of the German soldiers as they pulled him from his home. I turned toward the commotion in time to watch one soldier wrap his arms around the man, while he struggled to get free. The soldier held the man from behind, facing the other soldier. The first soldier pulled the man's arms back behind him and leaned back to give the other soldier a full frontal view of the man's face and body. Like a lumberjack with an axe, the other soldier drew his rifle, butt first, and reared back. The man saw what was coming, but had little time to react.

In a split second, the second German soldier planted the butt of his rifle squarely into the man's cheek. I heard the crack of his cheekbone when it shattered. The first soldier released the man, who fell face first into the street, his legs draped over the sidewalk. The soldiers looked down at him for a second. The soldier with the rifle prodded the man's lifeless body for a response. When none came, they looked up at each other with indifference, shook their heads, and made their way to the next house.

The soldiers continued to assemble the Jews into the street; the soldiers' faces spoke volumes, great confidence, arrogance, and disdain for their captives. We watched them direct the Jews to pick up dirt and horse manure with their bare hands from the streets and sidewalks. One soldier grabbed a man by the neck, dragged him to the ground, and plunged his face into a pile of manure. He turned back to his comrades, laughing with great pride. "I was just trying to help him get closer to his work," said the soldier. They all laughed. I looked up at my mother to help me make some sense of what I was witnessing. Her mouth fell open in disbelief, and her eyes welled up with tears. She could not understand what we witnessed any better than I could.

For every group of Jews kneeling on the ground, two or three soldiers conspired over which soldier would be next to humiliate their victims. They were pushed and beaten if they resisted or if they simply stood still. I was in shock. These were well-to-do families who provided work for many people in our community. Mama had cared for their children, and Babcia had cleaned their houses from time to time, especially in the winter when food was harder to come by.

One of the German soldiers who walked toward his truck made eye contact with me and stopped. I sheepishly looked away. Mama stepped closer to me and placed her hand on my shoulder. The soldier held his gaze on me for another second and then continued walking toward the truck. With concern for our own safety, we passed through town quickly and headed back home to Granice. On the way, we noticed Jewish country homes, here and there, which had been set on fire. The only thing left standing was the frame of the house.

Mama and Babcia learned that the Jews were being rounded up and detained in ghettos right outside of town, so the next day, we walked down the main path from our village to where they were held. When we arrived, it was strangely quiet. Two guards stood on either side of a long wire fence held up by two tall wooden posts. Barbed wire lined the fence top. The fencing looked a bit like chicken wire, except much stronger.

We got closer to the fence, and the guards saw us coming, but they did not leave their assigned post. Babcia led Mama and me to the side of the fence, away from the guards, so as not to engage them. When she approached the fence, Babcia recognized one of the women whose home she cleaned on occasion. They stood at the fence and talked. Others came to listen, eager to be part of a conversation with someone who was free, eager to learn anything they could about their impending fate. The poor souls looked like cats and dogs in a pet store window, who gather at the front of their cages hoping that you will be the one to bring them home with you.

"Don't worry. This can't last forever," Babcia consoled her. "This is all going to be worked out. You'll be released soon and be able to go back to your homes."

"I'm not so sure, Maria. I'm very worried. People are talking about what might become of us, and they're saying some horrible things. Do you see how the soldiers look at us? I'm afraid, Maria. I'm afraid."

Babcia and Mama tried in vain to comfort the woman. "Stay calm. This will all be over soon," they kept saying.

"Are they feeding you? Do you have enough to eat?"

"No. It's terrible. What they feed us is barely edible. And they laugh while we devour it, saying, we must be animals to eat things the pigs would never touch. Even then, it's only a few bites once a day. I'm so hungry, Maria. My stomach won't stop turning. It's only been a few days, but I can see how the hunger is beginning to affect some of us. It's terrible. It's terrible, Maria."

The woman continued to ramble. Her fingers held tightly onto the wire fence that separated us. She kept reaching for our hands as though it comforted her to touch someone on the "outside."

Babcia said, "Don't worry. We'll be back tomorrow and—"

"No, don't go!" the woman cried. "Please, please don't go."

The guard who was standing about thirty feet away looked in our direction with a stern expression.

"Don't worry." Babcia whispered. "We'll be back tomorrow and bring some bread for you and your family. We have to leave now." Babcia pulled away from the fence, working her hand out of the woman's grasp. With heavy hearts, we headed home.

We prayed so often during those uncertain times. For them. For ourselves. With the way the Jews were being treated, we wondered what fate held for us. Still, we kept visiting, bringing food, offering a few words of hope, maybe a tidbit of information on what might happen next. If nothing else, we brought a bit of encouragement and the feeling that someone on the outside cared.

After a few visits, however, a pair of German soldiers approached us and ordered, "Do not come here anymore." They told us, "Today it's the Jews' turn." He pointed at us. "If you disobey our orders, tomorrow it will be YOU!"

It was the last time we saw the Jews of Ropczyce.

CHAPTER 5
FAR FROM MY HOME

In the fall of 1940, my widowed American-born mother answered a knock at her front door. The person at the door handed her a notice from the German occupation government office or *Gmina*, as we called it in Polish. The letter stated that she was to report to the Gmina in Ropczyce immediately to address an urgent personal matter. When she arrived at the office, the counter clerk told her that she was scheduled to be shipped to Germany for farm work. Mama called it "free slave labor" for the German war effort.

Mama told them, "I can't go. I have a child."

They answered, "You can bring the child with you."

She said, "No, no. I'll stay here."

They responded, "You don't understand. We are not asking you to go. This is a direct government order. If you refuse, you and your daughter will be separated or will end up in prison for defying government orders."

We had no choice. Mama exchanged information with the government clerks and left with official papers in hand that instructed her where to report. Mama returned home to share the news with the family.

On the day we left, faces were serious and sad. There were few tears. Fear overtook all other emotions. Only Mama cried quietly while she went about the business of packing and loading the carriage. We left with a small bag of clothes. Mama left everything she owned to Babcia. Uncle John, my father's brother, took us to the train station with his horse and wagon.

From there, we were transported by train to a school in Krakow. The soldiers who met us were as cold as ice. They ordered us to follow a list of instructions that were handed to us, including a list of shots we were to receive, haircuts, and showers to disinfect us immediately on arrival.

It was a whirlwind from the minute we disembarked the train. Once again, from a distance, I saw German soldiers loading Jewish people on trucks, stealing their possessions, and burning their homes. They lit and threw explosives into the homes, which gutted the houses instantly.

We went through a series of inspections, sprayings, and health checks. The people administering the inspections performed their jobs like robots. They were straight-faced and tight-lipped, and gave one- or two-word orders: enough to make their instructions clear. I saw them depart from their assembly-line manner only once, when someone ahead of us became unruly. I watched the results of one woman's defiance, when she objected to having her body inspected.

"You can't treat us like animals," she screamed. "I won't be forced to take part in this!"

The reaction was swift and direct. The inspector raised her head, and a policeman immediately appeared. He grabbed the woman by the arm. She continued to rant and rave. With a closed fist, he beat her, his fist slamming into her face three or four times until her legs collapsed beneath her. The policeman dragged her to her feet, while spitting orders at her in Polish, "Stand up! Stand up, I said! You will do as you're told! Stand up and get back in line!"

Once she regained her composure, the inspection continued, and the policeman left in the same quick step with which he came.

The Germans cut off anyone's long hair and sprayed everyone's head for lice. We stood in single file and slowly approached the front of the line. I watched one woman, in particular, as she approached the inspectors with hair flowing down past the small of her back. They drew her hair away from her neck and began to cut. The long, cold and pointy shears made their way across the back of her neck, and the woman's lips trembled. Tears streamed down her face. She opened her mouth halfway, and streams of spit clung to her upper and lower lip. She cried, although no sound came out. I wondered why she was so distraught over having her hair cut. I was fine with my short hair, and Mama seemed comfortable with hers. Clearly she was crying over the fear of unknown things to come. At six years old, I took things as they appeared.

With our hair already at an acceptable length, Mama and I bypassed that stopping point and moved ahead to be sprayed for lice. One by one we were shoved into a shower with hundreds of naked women moaning, screaming, and crying. Frightened and embarrassed, I was reluctant to follow orders, especially because it involved entering a small, closed-off room, where all we could hear while waiting outside the door were blood-curdling screams. Mama insisted I do as they say.

A soldier entered the room from the other side and shouted orders in Polish to the women. "Move, you filthy animals!" he shouted when he grabbed hold of the arm of the first woman in line. She tumbled to the floor, and two women rushed to help her up. "Move, I said! I'm not going to stand here with you bitches any longer than I have to!"

In horror and shame, the women screamed and covered their bodies with their hands, trying in vain to minimize their humiliation. More women guards came into the room from each of the two entrances, pushing and pulling the women prisoners, all the while yelling for them to move faster. In a strange way, I found the experience to be interesting. With all that transpired during that short period, I didn't have time to digest what was really happening to us. I suppose any fear I did feel was minimized by the idea that, as my mother told me, "We'll be okay, as long as we do what they tell us," so I did what I was told, and kept turning this way and that to see all that was going on around me.

I had never seen a naked person before. It was quite an adventure for me. I even saw naked young boys in the showers, with eyes peeled wide open at the sight of the nude women. Polish-speaking German soldiers and civilian women were in charge of the showers. They spoke Polish perfectly. For all we knew, they may well have been Polish citizens, collaborating with the German government in fear for their lives.

After completing our list of instructions, we went to our room in the schoolhouse. A slate-faced man met us at the schoolhouse entrance where others, like us, were gathered. In a monotone voice and looking nowhere in particular, the man informed us, "Anyone who speaks out or is caught gathering in discussion will be quickly silenced."

We entered a room filled with people. Some secretly whispered, discussing the war, telling stories of what they had seen or what they heard had happened. I heard differing opinions of what was happening or what could happen. Except for those few solemn whispers, nobody spoke.

That night, after the chaos settled, we lay down on piles of straw strewn on the floor. I fell asleep to the nearby sounds of German shepherds barking. They barked day and night, and by nightfall my nerves were so numb from fear of them and the exhaustion from the day's ordeal that I drifted in and out of sleep until morning.

The next morning we awoke and were told to go outside and march. All of us, dressed in farm clothes, marched in groups, five by five, from place to place, surrounded by soldiers and their dogs. One woman always wore a kerchief on her head while we marched. One day we gathered in our group, assumed our normal cadence, and marched around the corner. While keeping pace with the others, the woman reached her hands up to untie her kerchief. She pulled it off her head, shook her hair free, and casually let the kerchief fall to the ground. Without a word to anyone, she simply stepped out of our line and strolled off. The soldiers never even noticed her. I suppose the fact that she walked so confidently and carefree diffused any concern the guards may have had. The things we recall as children!

A day later, the Germans shipped us on a smelly cattle train to Germany. Mama and I were allowed to bring one small suitcase for both of us. We were gathered like livestock, pushed and prodded, with more yelling and screaming by the soldiers. After our previous experience, almost everyone understood the routine and obediently fell into line. I looked around to see a familiar face or two. Surprisingly, I didn't recognize anyone from our village.

German soldiers dressed in dark olive green uniforms pointed at us to board the train. *"Mach schnell! Mach schnell!"*

We boarded the railcar as quickly as we could. I found it interesting that no matter how much they pushed, prodded, and yelled, it didn't make us move any faster. I got the sense that the soldiers enjoyed the power they exhibited. I could see it in their eyes. Every now and then, when they got tired of yelling, they pulled someone out of line to make an example of him or her. In line, about three people ahead of me, was a woman who looked to be in her thirties, with a small beaten-up satchel. I noticed her in particular because she didn't seem to be bothered by the yelling and screaming. She kept her place in line with a blank expression on her face.

One of the soldiers took notice and approached her. He got right up to her face, and in a barely audible tone said, "You worthless Polish scum. Are you stupid or just lazy?"

She never flinched or even looked up at him. At that, he broke into a tirade, demanding she move faster; his face never more than six inches from hers. He called her many terrible things. He used words I had never heard before.

He tried desperately to elicit some kind of reaction from her. When none came, he tore her bag away from her hand and rifled through it, announcing the contents to anyone who would listen, as though taking inventory. When he finished, he closed the satchel and threw it back in her direction. He turned and marched the few steps back to his perch where he could supervise. When the satchel landed, the contents sprayed out onto the dirt and gravel, and the woman quickly dropped to the ground to gather her belongings. The people behind her in line, including Mama and me, were not sure whether to wait for her to gather her things or bypass her in the line. Nobody had the nerve to stop to help her. We all froze. That's when chaos broke out.

"I said move!" The same soldier leaned toward us. "Are you all stupid? Maybe a cattle prod will help get things moving."

Mama followed the people in front of us, and moved slowly past the woman. She jerked my arm toward her to get my attention, and I took a few steps, my legs heading in one direction and my eyes still entranced by the chaos on the ground behind us. Some people danced in place. Others bumped into those who stood petrified. Eventually the woman rose to her feet, clutching her bag with clothing leaking out of every side, her body visibly trembling. The line resumed its pace.

We continued to make our way to the railcar entrance, shuffling our feet toward the head of the line. About ten or fifteen people stood ahead of us when the line stopped moving again. The railcar was full. One of the soldiers noticed we had stopped progressing, and he darted over to the front of our line.

He shoved the first few people away from the door. In a deep, booming voice, he bellowed into the railcar, "Everyone move to the back of the car! Move! Move! Move!" He stepped up to the railcar entrance and, like a lineman on a football team, lunged forward into the car; holding his rifle in both hands, horizontally across his body. The force of his momentum drove those at the front of the car backward, sandwiching those in the middle closer to each other and ultimately up against the opposing railcar wall.

The soldier then turned his attention toward us, at the front of the line. "Get in," he said sternly, slightly winded. We hesitated for a moment, not the slightest bit eager to enter the car, now bursting at the seams. "Move!" he demanded as he pulled the first two people by the arm and threw them in with the rest.

We boarded quickly. Thankfully we crossed the entrance last. When we stepped into the car, we turned to face the open doorway and draw one last breath of fresh air. We turned around in time to see the railcar door slide closed in front of us. We stood so close to the entrance that, when the door slammed shut, the steel handle scraped across my arm. The railcar had no windows. We stood in pitch darkness. I held on to Mama; at least that's whom I hoped I was holding. We stood so close to each other that I couldn't even lift my hand to scratch my head. Our eyes slowly adjusted to the darkness. From the cracks in the walls, I could see scarce traces of daylight. I was so little and surrounded by so many adults that when I looked up, aside from the wall in front of me, all I could see were stomachs and behinds. When I looked straight up, I saw the wooden ceiling and the tops of the walls.

The train pulled away, and I paid little attention as people talked among themselves. Young women who had never before been more than a mile or two from home wept. Others moaned. After an hour or so, the voices blended into a monotone mutter that lulled me in and out of sleep while I leaned on one adult or another through the hours of our long journey. We stood, nearly attached to each other, the entire time. With such close quarters, I found it difficult to breathe. Out of nervousness, some of the people smoked the few cigarettes they carried with them. The smoke choked off the air even more. We were packed like sardines. With no water or bathroom facilities, after a short while, we stunk like sardines, too. I smelled the stench of urine, feces, cigarette smoke, and sweaty skin rubbing against my own.

After about six hours, the train stopped at a field in eastern Germany. The door rolled open, and we were face to face with three German soldiers who told us to get off the train.

"*Aussteigen! Alle aussteigen!*" they shrieked in an unnatural tone.

Mama and I stood closest to the door, so we were first to get off. Because we had been in the dark for so long, the bright rays of the sun burned my eyes. My vision adjusted, and I looked around. Behind me and on either side were long lines of women and children hopping down from adjacent cattle cars, extending far in the distance.

A large number of German farmers approached the train. Looking us over, they picked their laborers, one by one. Heinrich was a tall and slim man with dark brown hair and a thin, clean-shaven face. He was a farmer in his forties wearing high black boots over his knees, and he held a stick. He pointed toward us with the stick, and we followed him to his horse and buggy.

The concentration and forced-labor camps of Nazi Germany were established in 1933 as a means of subverting those the Nazis believed to be political, ideological, or racial opponents of the Third Reich. With few exceptions, those who were sent to the concentration camps included "undesirables" who did not exhibit the characteristics of the preferred race. The list included Jews, POWs, gypsies, homosexuals, the disabled, criminals, and anyone who was sympathetic to any of these people. The Nazi concentration camps were separated into regions. Each region usually held the name of the primary camp within that region.

Between 1939 and 1945, at least 1.5 million Polish citizens were transported to the Reich for forced labor, many of them teenage boys and girls. Although Germany also used forced laborers from other places in Europe, those who were viewed as racially inferior, like the Poles, were subjected to intensified discriminatory measures. In many cities, they were forced to live in segregated barracks behind barbed wire. Social relations with Germans outside work were forbidden, and sexual relations ("racial defilement") were considered a capital crime punishable by death.[9]

I read a good description of how the camps were categorized. Moshe Lifshitz described the division of the Nazi camps as follows:

- Labor camps: concentration camps where interned inmates had to perform hard physical labor under inhuman conditions and cruel treatment. Some of these camps were sub-camps of bigger camps, or "operational camps," established for a temporary need.
- Transit and collection camps: camps where inmates were collected and routed to main camps or temporarily held
- POW camps: concentration camps where prisoners of war were held after capture. These POWs endured torture and liquidation on a big scale.

- Camps for rehabilitation and re-education of Poles: camps where the intelligentsia of the ethnic Poles were held and re-educated in light of German-Nazi values as slaves.
- Hostage camps: camps where hostages were held and killed as reprisals
- Extermination camps: these camps were built to systematically kill, usually by gassing.[10]

Although none of the categories is independent, each camp could be classified as a mixture of several of the above, and all camps had some of the elements of an extermination camp. Still, systematic extermination of new arrivals occurred in specific camps.[10]

Heinrich brought us to a village about two hours outside of Dresden, where he owned a large farm in that area. It included an asphalt and cement factory. What we didn't know at that time was that we were part of the notorious Buchenwald network of camps. The village was a dot on the map, a quiet farm community nestled in a dense forest. It had no store. One main road passed through the village that was surrounded by small mountains and a few lakes. Geese and ducks swam and flew here and there. Brooks and streams meandered across some of the fields, and a small river provided energy for the flour mill, which sat on its east bank. Everything in the village appeared to be in its proper place, almost like a movie set.

When we arrived at the farm, Heinrich steered the carriage toward a courtyard, which we entered through a huge wooden gate. The gate was big enough for tractors and machinery to pass through, and it was always left open during the day. In the middle of the courtyard was a pile of manure. On the left of the courtyard stood a huge barn to store hay. To the right, a horse stable held about eight or ten horses. On top of the horse stable was an apartment that housed a German woman. She was about seven months pregnant, and her husband was in the German military. When we arrived, I saw her children, a boy and a girl, playing in the yard. They looked to be about five and three years old, respectively. I remarked at how neatly dressed they were, in comparison to me. The girl wore a simple light blue dress, and the boy wore a dark pair of pants and a shirt. As much as was happening to us at that moment, I took a particular interest in the children because, by then, my opportunities to play were few. My inability to speak German didn't improve my prospects for acquiring playmates.

We climbed down from the carriage. Other Polish and Russian prisoners were already hard at work by the time we got there. The dust that was kicked up by the horse's hooves and the wheels of the buggy still hung in the air. We stood for only a moment to look around before Heinrich motioned for us. We followed Heinrich through the courtyard and were met by his wife, Olga. Olga was pleasant, but not overly friendly. She stood tall and slim, with dark-colored clothes and a light-colored apron. She wore her dark brown hair up in a bun.

Olga directed us to our living quarters. We had one room on the first floor of a large white wood-planked house with many rooms. By comparison to what I was used to in Poland, the house was in slightly better condition. Our room had a single window that looked out into the courtyard. The washroom beneath our living quarters in the basement was where we all went to clean off at the end of the day. Tubs and a wood-burning stove to heat the water were available there for common use by all of the workers living in the house. We also washed our clothes there by hand, of course.

There were three beds with down covers in our room. Two were against the back wall, and one stood in the middle of the room. Mama showed me to the bed on the right, near the door, and said, "That one is ours." The room had no running water, bathrooms, or heat. We shivered a lot during the winter. Thank goodness for our down comforters. I recall the ritual of blowing hot air under my covers to stay warm. It eventually took the chill off. Still, I was awakened many times during those wintry nights by my body's spastic shivering brought on by the bitter cold against my bare skin.

Our outhouse was across the courtyard, near the horse stable. All the workers used it. It had no toilet paper, though. Curiously, toilet paper was a luxury I was never exposed to in all my years in

Poland or Germany. Now, more than sixty years later, I don't know how we survived without it.

After a short time, we were surprised to see Aunt Julia and Mama's best friend, Janina, arrive at the camp. There was a comfort that came from sharing our unspoken misery with family and friends; probably because we knew they cared. Their presence eased our tension a little. We were not exactly sure how they ended up at the same camp, but we were not allowed to question or inquire. Mama suppressed her outward expression of happiness, and I followed her example, to avoid drawing attention to ourselves. They were there, it was good, and that was all. Although Aunt Julia lived with us in the same room throughout our time at the large farm, Janina disappeared a few months following her arrival. We never saw her again.

It took about ten minutes to walk to Heinrich and Olga's house from our room. To get there, we passed the well, which was our source for drinking water. Also along the way, a small stream meandered across the grounds and another well-maintained, freshly painted farmhouse stood nearby. Through another wooden gate into a courtyard, we passed stables that held many cows and pigs that never left the barn.

Each morning, Mama and the others reported to work, usually at about six. For the first few weeks that Mama headed for the fields with the other workers, I felt paralyzed by anxiety and fear. Being a six-year-old left all alone in a strange place with no knowledge of the language took some getting used to. To keep me occupied, and after she became comfortable with her routine, Mama gave me little tasks to do. Each evening before dark, I took Heinrich's big black boots down to the river and washed off the dirt and mud that gathered on them during the workday. Mama also instructed me to make sure she had water that she could use to wash off when she came home from the fields. She gave me a pail and showed me how to draw water from the well using a rope I tied to the pail handle. It wasn't a big responsibility, but it made me feel useful.

One day at the well, I tied the rope to the pail and released the squeaky crank handle to lower the pail down to the water. When the crank stopped turning, I didn't hear the pail hit bottom, so the thought struck me, *"Just how far was that pail traveling?"* With nobody around to answer my question, I resolved to find the answer myself. I pulled myself up onto the stone well wall. Holding the well crank handle with one hand and the top of the stone wall with the other, I maneuvered my upper body onto the top of the well wall. With my feet dusting the ground, I pushed myself high enough to lean my upper body over the edge and look in.

As children, we sometimes have no idea of the precarious situations we place ourselves in until it's too late. As a result, our ignorance allows for a few more liberties with safety than we might otherwise permit. I flung my face forward with great enthusiasm, and my curiosity was immediately satisfied. All at once, my heart pounded through my chest in double time, adrenaline poured through my veins, and I thought, *"This was probably not such a good idea."* My arms stiffened in shock. I awkwardly gripped to gain a better hold of the well and crank handle. The sudden jerk of my body pulled me off balance. I came dangerously close to a fifty-foot dive into a dark, wet hole.

With head spinning and feet dangling in the air, I pushed myself as hard as I could away from the center of the hole and slid back over the outside edge of the well, landing safely on solid ground. I stood for a minute, my legs shaking and my mouth hanging open in disbelief. Had I fallen in, nobody would have ever known or even begun to look for me until nighttime, when Mama returned from the fields. With almost everyone at work in the fields, nobody was around to even wonder what might have happened to me.

I snapped out of it and returned to my task, cranking the well handle, which slowly lifted the full pail of water closer and closer to me. It took a while before I learned exactly how far down the pail traveled into the well. Until then, knowing that it was "very far" was good enough for me.

A few weeks went by, and Heinrich and Olga introduced me to their daughter Gretchen, who had arrived home from boarding school the day before. We met in the courtyard. Gretchen was about twelve; maybe fourteen. She was a tall, slender, pretty girl with dark brown hair. Gretchen lived away at school most of the time, so I saw her only a few times a year. I was too young to play with her, but when she came home, I sometimes found myself watching her from a distance while she played with her friends. We talked occasionally. She seemed to be a nice girl, kind and always pleasant.

CHAPTER 6
SLAVE LABORERS

At Heinrich's farm, we were fed bread and soup, mostly cabbage soup, which we carefully inspected for the customary dead fly or two. We sat on wooden benches and ate in groups, saying almost nothing, although plenty was on our minds. We got skinnier by the day. With as hard as the adults worked, our one meal each day never satisfied our hunger. The first time we sat down to eat, I looked around at the others with whom we sat. The helpless look of hunger on each human face depressed me. I suppose I didn't look much better to them.

Mama had to milk cows, remove manure, and lay fresh straw for the cows every day at the stable. She kept the area clean. She pushed the manure and straw using a shovel and wheelbarrow, day after day. She frequently complained about the pain in her wrist and arms.

As the war progressed, German youth trained to become loyal Nazi soldiers. With all of the adult males and their sons involved in the war to varying degrees, fewer and fewer men were available to work the fields, so Germany secured more forced laborers from other occupied countries to work their farms, factories, and fields. Heinrich's farm had all sorts of modern farm equipment we had never seen before. Mama had to learn how to drive a tractor and operate various types of machinery. She performed these tasks in addition to her other duties.

One time the tractor broke down. Without the tractor, the workers could not bring the wagon full of hay into the barn, so they brought over a bull to pull the wagon. They wrapped a rope around the bull's neck and led him to the wagon, where they jostled him into position to hook him up. The bull had other plans. Once he realized he was going to have to work, the bull became less cooperative. The workers tried everything make him move. They pushed him. They pulled him. They offered him grass. They smacked him on the behind. Nothing worked. He refused to budge. Finally, as a last resort, someone put a hot cigarette under the bull's tail. Like a rocket, the bull took off down the road with the wagon rambling along behind him and the workers in hot pursuit. He bypassed the barn and kept going in full gallop toward the next village before the wagon tipped over; bringing his free reign to an end. Did we ever laugh!

At the end of any normal day, the workers put away their tools and headed back to their rooms against the backdrop of a setting sun. Exhausted and preoccupied, nobody paid any attention to what I was up to, so as I often did, I wandered off toward anything that captured my interest. One time my eye caught sight of a tractor that sat off the main grounds along the edge of the forest. One of the workers had jumped off of it only a moment ago, and was headed back to his room.

I made my way toward the tractor and listened to it cool down, knocking and pinging as I approached. I studied the details of its shape: the intricate engine, the worn, brown leather seat, and the huge black rubber tires with treads so deep I could fit my hand inside. I touched my fingers to the engine to feel the warmth radiating from it and quickly pulled my hand back when the hot steel seared my fingertips. I walked around to the back to study the depth of the tire treads. The treads were filled with soil and what looked like, yes, it was a potato! A fresh, ripe potato! My mouth watered. I debated over and over, loud enough for only the forest chipmunks to hear, "Should I take it? Should I take it? Should I?"

I looked around to see if anyone was watching and quickly dug through the dirt to dislodge the potato from deep in the tire tread.

The dirt fell from the tire, and revealed another potato. I picked that one, and still another potato appeared. I lifted the potato to my mouth to take a bite, and the thought occurred to me, *"Could I get sick from eating a raw potato?"* I wasn't sure, but even as hungry as I was, I wasn't willing to take the chance. I looked up again, to ensure nobody saw the treasure I had discovered and hurriedly gathered a few of my findings into my dress. Setting the remaining potatoes off to the side, hidden under some nearby leaves, I smuggled each one, one by one, into our room for Mama and me to discreetly cook on the wood-burning stove and eat later.

Besides the Polish and Russian civilian workers on the farm, Heinrich had French and Russian prisoners of war working at the nearby rock quarry. Stone by stone, they disassembled a mountain to make asphalt for the road. There, behind the barbed-wire fence, they worked, day after day. They hammered away at the stones with their pick axes and shovels. Their fingers and hands bled through their dry, dirt-stained skin and the remnants of their work lodged beneath their cracked, overgrown fingernails. These same prisoners laid the asphalt to turn the dirt paths of our small community into a paved road.

I don't know where they were housed. I saw them simply appear every morning. Like a child enjoys standing on the sidewalk to marvel at a passing parade, I watched these pathetic souls make their way to work each day.

One Monday morning (I remember it was Monday, because it was the day after our lighter workday), the guards assembled the POWs in groups of twenty, and they marched in formation to the quarry. The men were ragged. Skinny and unhealthy in appearance, they kept a surprisingly good cadence, as weak and hungry as they must have been. Starved as we were, I could only imagine how hungry they must have been. That day, however, was different. My stomach was still full from my potato feast the day before, and so many discarded potatoes remained at the edge of the forest that I had more than enough to share.

That's when the idea struck me. As the German soldiers marched the prisoners by our gate, I could quietly slip the prisoners a potato or two that I held in my stash. The only problem with my plan was that armed German soldiers guarded the prisoners while they marched, and they would scarcely approve of my generosity. Two guards flanked each side of the POWs, stationed about midway down the marching line. *"How could I get past them?"* I wondered. I stood there staring, determined to figure out how to give the prisoners some of my food.

With nothing else nearly as interesting to do, I waited for an opportunity. The first group of twenty POWs passed by me, while other groups assembled in the distance. The second and third group passed me. I saw only two more groups assembling, and my heart raced. When the last group of twenty passed me, I took a deep breath and ran up to the last prisoner in line. I tugged at the back of his shirt. He turned around and looked down at me in amazement. His pace drifted slowly away from the others, and I lifted my arm to hand him my potato, while I jogged to keep up with him. With eyes wide open, he reached for the potato and quickly pressed it against his leg. I think I caught him off guard. He was so overcome at the sight of it that, when I placed it in his hand, it bounced around in his fingers for a split second. I thought he would drop it.

He finally wrapped his fingers firmly around the potato and hastily regained the tempo of his group's cadence. The prisoner said nothing. He continued past me with not so much as a smile, for fear of getting caught. My heart pounded through my shirt, but I felt proud of myself. I stood in the middle of the courtyard for a second. The group continued on its way, the dust kicking up with every step.

The next day I stood at the same gate at the same time and waited with another potato concealed in my dress. Again the prisoners fell into line and headed toward me in measured tempo at the order of the German soldier in charge. As they approached, I saw the prisoner from the day before assembling in the same marching position within the same group as the day before. At about one hundred feet from each other, I can't say I actually saw his eyes clearly enough to know that he stared at me, but his body language told me that our eyes were locked on each other.

The soldier in charge gave the order and my prisoner's group marched. Once again, the closer he got, the harder my heart pounded. I inched closer to their pathway, to minimize my steps. My nervous hands dripped with perspiration from my anxious exhilaration. When he got within fifteen feet of me, we exchanged an intense stare. I pondered the consequences of my actions while the group drew closer. The simple act of transferring a potato from my hand to his fueled an intense adrenaline rush. Seconds passed, and the sweat from my hands permeated the potato. What was once a hard, dense object became like putty in my moist hand.

The men drew still closer. Closer. Closer. I waited for precisely the right moment. My heartbeat raced. Even so, I was a little more confident than the last time. *"Now!"* I said to myself. I stepped forward to hand the prisoner my potato. This time we made the exchange as though we had practiced it for weeks. He passed me, and I detected a subtle smile from him, along with a word of thanks. *"Danke,"* he said.

During that period, the French prisoners were allowed to receive small packages from France. To my surprise, after a few potato deliveries, the prisoner took my potato and handed me something wrapped in paper. I took it, hid it in my dress, and raced back to our room. I had never seen chocolate before, but it didn't take me long to develop a taste for the heavenly treat. Over time, the prisoners told me that even potato peels would be appreciated. I brought them whatever I could.

One afternoon I was out in the courtyard, walking around with little to do. A few of the German and Polish foremen's kids, four boys and a girl, approached me. All looked to be between ten and twelve. One of them was more confident than the others. He appeared to be the oldest, and he asked most of the questions.

"What are you doing?" he inquired. I noticed a mischievous look on their faces.

"Nothing," I responded guardedly.

"Why don't you come and play with us?" he suggested.

I should have known they were up to something, but I was terribly lonely and desperately wanted to believe that some of the neighborhood children would play with me.

"Come on," they yelled to me while running toward the chicken coop. The oldest boy led the way, followed by the others. I thought for a minute, but when they turned the corner, I decided to join them, running as fast as I could to catch up.

We stopped at the entrance to the chicken coop, all of us panting for air from the jog.

"What's your name?" the foreman's oldest son inquired in Polish.

"Cecylia," I said, not being confident enough to ask any questions of my own.

"What's it like to live in those shacks that you people live in?" he asked.

The boys giggled in the background.

"It's okay," I said sheepishly in a kind of singsong voice. I looked down at our feet when we spoke, remarking that they wore shoes, and I didn't, having recently outgrown mine. If I wasn't embarrassed enough by their questions, my bare feet were certainly enough to cause my palms to sweat.

"How come your hands are so dirty? Don't you ever wash?" More giggling.

I felt my cheeks heat up with embarrassment. Still, I tried to maintain the dialogue.

I laughed politely to appear part of the group. "Sure, I do. I usually wash off at the end of the day. My hands are dirty because I was playing in the yard. They're never this dirty," I fibbed.

One of the boys leaned toward me coyly. "Do you have any friends? I see you out in the courtyard all the time, just roaming around doing nothing."

I stood silent; trying to think of something to say. The boy continued before I could respond. "You know, if you took a bath once in a while and wore some decent clothes, maybe someone would take pity on you and play with you." They roared in laughter, and my eyes welled with tears. Like a shark who can detect the smallest drop of blood, the boy pounced on my display of weakness. "My father says you people are useless, just good-for-nothing Polish swine. And . . . ewwwww," he leaned closer. "You smell just as bad."

The laughter continued.

"She smells just like chicken shit!"

"Maybe that's what she is … chicken shit!"

"Well, what is she doing out here? She belongs with the rest of the manure." At that, the oldest boy came toward me and wrapped his arms around my upper body, gluing my arms to my sides. He dragged me toward the chicken coop entrance, and one of the boys swung the coop door open. Kicking wildly, I tried to dig my heels into one of his feet, forcing him to let me go, but I was no match for him.

The boy flung me into the coop, and I landed on the ground, face first. Chickens scattered nervously and clucked loudly as they ran. I looked back at the entrance, only to see them hurriedly latch the door.

One of the boys announced, "Boy, it smells so much better now that the chicken shit has been put back where it belongs." They ran off with great pride and glee, having amused themselves at my expense.

I found myself surrounded by hundreds of clucking chickens, and the smell was unbearable. The gasses coming from the manure choked off the air. I could hardly breathe. I darted around from wall to wall like a caged animal, searching for a way out. I ran from side to side, down the long corridor along the wooden shelves covered in straw, where the chickens laid their eggs. Up and down, I searched for a doorway to escape, but couldn't find one. Another idea came to mind. I could break through the wall with something, anything. I searched nervously, on my hands and knees, for a stray piece of wood or metal, and found nothing but dirt and chicken manure.

Out of breath, I stood there and thought, *"How will Mama find me? What if I can't get out? What do I do? What do I do?"* Anxiety was overtaking me. When I exhausted all my options for escaping, I plopped down in the corner of the chicken coop. I draped my arms over my raised knees, lowered my head into my hands, and cried.

After a while, I heard some rustling at one end of the chicken coop. I raised my head slowly to look in that direction. The last few tears slipped off my cheeks into my lap. When my eyes dried and my vision cleared, I noticed the chickens had settled down and were coming out of their hiding place. They clucked in a muffled tone and made their way cautiously in my direction. I watched as they moved slightly closer, then back, testing the waters, for fear I might begin another of what they perceived to be a reckless endeavor.

The more I sat and watched them, the calmer they became. With nothing else to do, I continued to watch them and they went back to their usual routine of clawing and pecking at the ground. That's when I saw something surprising. One of the chickens was miraculously outside the coop! I gasped, and the chickens whirled around to look at me. "How did you get out there, chicky?" I spoke to her in a softer tone. I sat still so as not to agitate the others, calling to the lone chicken to come back the same way she left. "How did she get out there?" I exclaimed in a hushed tone.

In my despair, I hadn't noticed the small gap at the other end of the chicken coop, between the base of the coop's wooden wall and the ground. It was barely large enough for a chicken to pass through, but *"I think I can make it through,"* I said to myself with great enthusiasm. I raced over to the opening, scattering chickens left and right. I slid down onto the ground. I pushed my shoulders up to the opening and realized it was way too small. Still, with no other options, I thought I'd give it a try anyway.

I lifted my hands over my head and crawled toward the opening. Wriggling and twisting along the ground, inching my way along, I tried to squeeze through. I couldn't fit. I inched back and wracked my brain for other options, but that opening seemed like the only way out. I then tried head first, pushing myself out with my hands underneath me. Of course, I was a little bigger than a chicken.

I inched closer along the ground and slowly made my way a little bit farther. I moved along through the narrow opening, and I could feel the rough wooden boards combing my back and sides. They scraped my skin, but it didn't matter. I was making progress. Over and over, I pushed with my fingers and toes through the dirt like a caterpillar. It worked! I was finally moving forward! However slowly, I was still moving forward. My heart raced as my emotions fluttered between the exuberance of a successful escape and the thought of being discovered pinned beneath the chicken coop wall. I continued to push forward. The distance wasn't far, but it was taking forever, given my caterpillar crawl.

My breathing quickened, and sweat dripped from my forehead. A few of the beads of sweat meandered down across the bridge of my nose and into my eyes. While the water droplets burned my eyes and blurred my vision, my focus was so intently fixed on the fresh air outside the coop that I refused to let it affect my momentum.

I dragged and twisted my hips through the opening and was jerked backward. I pulled forward, but something was holding me back. I jerked my body forward again, but I couldn't move. Without a clear view behind me, it took a few minutes to realize that my dress had caught a stray nail which kept me from moving. I closed my eyes and sighed. *"So close, but not quite,"* I thought. I stopped for a moment and visualized how to caterpillar crawl in reverse. Over and over, I worked my way backwards and then forward until finally the dress tore away from the nail, and I moved along to freedom.

I headed back to our room, relieved. I stepped across the threshold, and the hunger pangs that gnawed at my stomach every single day returned, so I went back into the coop and knelt at the entrance from which I had managed to escape only moments before. *"Is it worth another trip through the obstacle course in exchange for the chance to make the hunger pangs go away for a while?"* I wondered. *"You bet it is!"* I decided.

I looked around to confirm that nobody could see me, and having become an expert at the caterpillar crawl, I made my way back inside the coop. Once inside, I slowly walked over to the beds of straw where the chickens were nesting. In slow motion, so as not to alarm the chickens, I slid my hand between a chicken and the straw, in search of an egg. The minute I touched the chicken she clucked loudly, and I pulled my hand away as a reflex.

I looked around again. Nobody there. Once more I reached under the chicken to grab an egg. This time, her clucking didn't stop me. I reached around for a second to get a good grip on an egg and then quickly pulled back from the chicken with my prize in hand. I held it for a moment in both hands; looking at it as though it were made of gold.

I poked a hole in the eggshell and sucked out the treat inside. It went down smoothly and immediately quelled my hunger. My body tingled with satisfaction. The feeling was invigorating, and like a drug addict, I had to have more. After three eggs and a full tummy, I headed back to our room.

As much as I would have liked, I could not bring any eggs for Mama. I would have had to maneuver them through that tiny opening and across the courtyard without anyone seeing. I couldn't do it. If caught stealing, I would have been severely punished, which could have included beatings or separation from my mother. Even so, I did muster courage enough to go back to the chicken coop a few more times before I outgrew the entrance.

After some months, Mama asked Heinrich if she could send her daughter to school. Heinrich told us that if we became German citizens, only then would we be allowed to do everything the Germans did. Mama emphatically told Heinrich, "I am an American citizen, and I will die an American!"

Heinrich warned her not to speak so boldly. "You may well die an American. The Germans are fighting the Americans, and continued talk like that could create serious trouble for you and your daughter."

Heinrich allowed us to move freely throughout the farm, and in some cases even around town, with permission. It was clear that any attempts to escape would be met with severe punishment. Although some people did, Mama never discussed escape as an option. The risks appeared too great.

One Easter Sunday, some of the Polish workers were allowed to attend Mass. About ten of us walked a few miles down the road into town, to the Catholic Church. We approached the building, climbed the steps, and slowly opened the large wooden door. The church was about half full, and the priest was beginning his sermon. We stood quietly in the back, hoping nobody would notice us. The priest spoke to his congregation, and then abruptly stopped when he caught sight of our group. He quietly stepped down from the pulpit and walked to the back of the church. It was an awkward moment. All eyes turned in our direction, as the priest headed toward us. He stood in front of us and whispered, "Please, all of you must leave immediately. If you don't, they'll close down this church."

We stood silent for a minute. He looked at us with an expression of helplessness. The consequences of what the priest said finally sank in. We acknowledged his request, genuflected in the direction of the altar, and turned to leave with tear-filled eyes.

Ashamed and dejected, we headed back to the camp. We became painfully aware at how much our appearance made us stand out. We were dirty and unkempt. Our clothing was tattered and old. Most of us wore the same clothes we had worn upon arriving at the camp, months before. Others were given badly worn hand-me-downs from nearby German families. To degrade us even further, all of us were forced to wear a letter "P" on our clothing to clearly identify us as Poles. In retrospect, to think that we could possibly blend in anywhere the way we looked only proved how desperately we wanted to believe we could.

One Sunday afternoon, the only day of reduced work, the grounds were relatively quiet. A group of us gathered to sing, dance, and play the harmonica in one of the workers' rooms. The bright sunshine lifted everyone's spirits, creating an uncharacteristically jovial tone in the courtyard. When someone suggested the idea of a little social pastime to the few of us standing around, it seemed like a harmless way to take advantage of a beautiful day. A handful of us made our way toward the room, inviting one or two others along the way. It didn't take many people to fill the room, which was a little bit smaller than ours, with a single bed against each wall. I stood close to the door and watched the adults sing songs I had heard, but didn't know well. The music played and I looked around, taking note of each person and their unique personality. Aunt Julia and Mama were talking, singing, and having a good time. To their right, the harmonica player sat on the bed and kept time with his foot. He was short with light brown hair, and he blew into his instrument with great pride.

About five men and five or six women joined together. One of the men, Andrzej, lived a few rooms from ours, and I frequently saw him around the grounds. He was a tall, skinny man with a Clark Gable mustache that had a yellow tint from the huge volume of cigarettes he consumed. With as few resources as we had, I often wondered how he was always able to find something to smoke. He wasn't picky. If it burned, he smoked it.

After about an hour, we heard the rumble of motorcycles from outside the open window. We stopped singing, and a few in the group went over to the window to see what the commotion was on such a quiet Sunday. Dressed in ominous black uniforms, the Nazi secret state police, particularly well known for their brutality, had pulled into the courtyard. Curious to find out where they were headed, some of the adults moved toward the door to go outside and find out. One of the women reached for the door, and it burst open. Two Gestapo agents exploded into the room. They were slim, good-looking young men of medium height. One of them was clean shaven. The other had a dark mustache. Their eyes filled with rage as they looked us over.

Each Gestapo agent set his sights on one of the men in our party. Without saying a word, they moved toward their selected targets. Andrzej and I were facing each other, when one of the agents stepped in front of me and lunged toward Andrzej. The agent struck him in the face with the closed fist of a black-gloved hand. Andrzej's head twirled to the left, and the momentum forced him from the bed where he sat. With one hand, he caught himself before he landed on the floor.

Andrzej quickly pushed himself up to a standing position, although bent over, and the agent moved in to expel the rage he had built up. With Andrzej still hunched, the agent kicked him so hard

I heard Andrzej's ribs crack. Andrzej fell over onto his back, and the agent moved in closer to continue his assault. Andrzej slowly sat up, holding his side, still trying to regain his balance and fend off the punches as they flew. He rolled over onto his knees in a final attempt to stand, and I watched the agent cock his arm back and forth quickly, hitting Andrzej repeatedly in the face and neck.

Blood sprayed from Andrzej's mouth, and the agent continued to bludgeon him. Andrzej tried, in vain, to hold the agent at bay and maintain some sense of dignity while the pummeling continued. Finally, Andrzej fell to the ground like a load of laundry. He had barely enough energy to lift his hands over his head to protect himself from any further beating. The agent stopped and stood over him, wiping the sweat from his forehead, his chest heaving, panting for air from the workout.

The other agent charged past me and headed toward one of the other men in our party, leading the way with the butt of his rifle. The rifle met its target. Teeth went flying, and blood spattered when the man caromed off the back wall. He lifted his arms to protect his face as best he could. Dazed, the man awkwardly scrambled to maintain his balance and some degree of composure, using the wall to hold himself up. The agent continued to beat him with his gloved fist and black shiny boot until the man finally fell to the ground. His blood, smeared high on the wall, was a reminder that he was, at one time, standing during the ordeal.

We all watched helplessly. Everything happened fast, but the adults moved in front of me to shield me from the aftereffects. I didn't mind not seeing. I couldn't bear to watch anymore.

"You were warned not to gather in groups when you arrived here," said one of the agents. "Conspirators will not be tolerated in this camp!"

The Gestapo left as quickly as they came. The men dragged themselves off the floor. They endured the physical pain by themselves, but we all shared in the embarrassment and emotional distress of that incident.

The men wiped the blood from their faces, and we whispered, "Who called them? Who could it have been?" We watched the agents board their motorcycles and dash away in a cloud of dust. We hurried back to our own room, still wondering, "Who could have done this?" Although we were never able to prove it, the general belief was always that the Polish foreman, Tomasz, had called them to solidify his loyalty to his German boss. From that point on, we were more careful.

As time passed, Olga grew fond of me and periodically invited me to her house to play her piano. The first time she extended the invitation, it surprised me, because I found her general demeanor toward me to be quite cool. Regardless, excitement overtook my apprehension, and I happily followed her back to her house.

Their home was adorned with bright-colored flowers that hung in wooden planters outside each window. The inside of her house was handsomely decorated. Dark wooden chairs, rich in color, accented the entrance. Each room displayed a distinctly ornate dresser and perfectly tailored curtains. We entered the house into a long, thin hallway. Down the hall on the left stood a set of stairs that led up to their bedrooms. On the right, doorways opened up to two rooms separated by the kitchen. The largest room in the house, probably used to entertain guests, had a sliding wall that could convert the single room into two smaller ones. I tried to hide my amazement. To a young, poor Polish girl, the experience was fascinating. I had never seen anything like it. My wide eyes and half-open mouth offered Olga a compliment that no words could match.

The piano sat along the wall on the left side of the big room. Olga prompted me to sit and play. I happily obliged, improvising all the Polish songs I could recall. On most visits to Olga's house, the radio played softly in the background. I had never seen a radio before, and after growing more comfortable in Olga's house, I asked if she would give me one. "Oh, no," she replied. "You are not allowed. You are not German." The radio played soothing, classical music, often by German composers, Bach and Wagner, whom Olga so proudly identified as though they were close friends. The music was a frequent prelude to the broadcast of Hitler's screaming and shrieking speeches. The abrupt transition from the calming symphony annoyed me. I paid little attention to what Hitler said, because at my age, I couldn't comprehend much of the political brainwashing he spewed. I only remarked to myself at what an unusually shrill voice he had. At the time, we certainly had no idea that his genocidal plans were well under way.

One time Olga went into the nearby washroom to take a sponge bath. She told me not to let anyone into her studio. "Okay," I said. After a while, I tiptoed over to her studio door. Pretending to be an adult, I clomped with my heaviest feet, step by step, toward her washroom. In my deepest German voice, I bellowed a few words to get her attention.

I listened intently. I heard the sound of water frantically swishing around in the other room. I giggled a little and heard her jump out of the bath, scurrying to get her robe. She hurried out of the bathroom to find me standing at the studio door; slightly embarrassed at my inability to contain my laughter. After her frantic expression changed to relief, we shared a good laugh. I played that trick on her from time to time after that. Even though she knew it was me calling out to her, we always laughed when she came running.

One summer morning at sunrise, Tomasz, the Polish foreman, gathered the workers in the courtyard and told them they weren't producing enough, and they had to work harder. Mama spoke up and said, "We can barely survive on what you're feeding us. Feed us more, and we'll be able to produce more." The next morning, before six o'clock, Mama got up to report to the courtyard with the other workers for their daily work orders. I lay in bed. Instead of the light from the nearby window waking me, I arose to the sounds of loud voices from outside in the courtyard. I heard Mama's voice and then a man's voice that overshadowed hers. I listened closely, but couldn't make out what they were saying.

The tone of the man's voice, however, was unmistakable. He was yelling at Mama. The sound of his voice scared me. I peeked out from one side of the attic window and looked down over the courtyard. From there I could see Mama standing face to face with

Tomasz. Other workers stood by awaiting their work orders for the day. Some hung around for no other reason than to watch Mama get scolded. The veins in Tomasz's neck bulged as he screamed at Mama in what seemed to be a never-ending tirade over something having to do with "food and work." I couldn't really follow the conversation.

Without warning, the foreman reared back and punched Mama directly in the mouth. With a back and forth motion, he continued to slap her. Mama screamed and covered her face with her hands to deflect the punishment. The initial expression on Mama's face was one of disbelief.

I hurried down the stairs shrieking, "Mama! Mama! What is he doing to you?" I jumped from the last few steps and ran out the door into the courtyard. Mama lay on the ground curled up in a ball with Tomasz standing over her. When I approached, Tomasz stopped hitting Mama, but he maintained his steely-eyed focus on her.

When Mama saw me, she collected herself and rose to her feet; appearing even more embarrassed by the idea that her daughter should have to see her in such a condition. She looked up, and I saw blood flowing from her face. I screamed even louder and ran to help her up.

"I'll be okay. I'll be okay. Go back to bed," she said softly. She tried to wipe the blood from her face.

I looked at my mother with blood smeared all over her hands, her face, her white blouse, and skirt. I glanced at the foreman for an instant, with his stern eyes still fixed on my mother, not saying a word. He turned and left the courtyard; his boots stomping the ground as he stormed off. Mama quickly cleaned herself up and again told me to go back to bed. She went off to the fields for the day, and I lay in bed staring at the ceiling with tears flowing onto my pillow.

Mama was never the same after that. It seemed as though that beating took all of the life out of her. When she returned home that night, she explained what caused the foreman to get so angry. "When we gathered in the courtyard," Mama began, "instead of giving each of us our work orders, Tomasz told us all that we weren't working hard enough. I shouldn't have said a word, but I spoke up in our defense. 'If you feed us better,' I told him, 'we'll get stronger and be able to work harder.' As soon as I said it, I wished I could have taken it back. People moved away as Tomasz stepped toward me. He said I was trying to interfere with the work at the labor camp. 'Sabotage' was the word he used, and 'your behavior will not be tolerated.'" Mama later told me the beating hurt twice as much because the foreman was Polish.

Besides feeding us soup and bread, Heinrich occasionally killed a pig and had small sausages made from the scrap meat. When the sausages were packed and cooked, the children often stood by, hoping to receive a morsel or two. I was quick to hold out my hand. Like sea gulls, the few children who surrounded Heinrich hovered in anticipation of an indulgence that, for me, came only on rare occasion. Once a tidbit was clutched in my fingers, I ran off to a quiet place to savor the moment. Each bite of the warm, juicy, tender treat was a euphoric experience as it passed over my taste buds. I took extra small bites to make the experience last longer. Unfortunately it did little to help the hunger pangs subside.

The war made its way closer to us. Sometimes at night, from the hilltop near the farm, we'd watch the sights and sounds of Allied bombs as they exploded over the larger nearby German cities, if the weather cooperated. From a distance, I saw an occasional ball of fire light up the distant sky.

During the day, German soldiers and youth groups sang and marched to the beat of pounding drums, practicing to become good, loyal Nazis. The German children followed in the footsteps of their parents. As most children do, they listened to their parents' conversations around the kitchen table and imitated their behaviors, attitudes, and general manner. That behavior was reflected in the German children's treatment of the Polish kids.

One hot summer afternoon, a group of older German kids invited me to come to the lake with them.

"I can't swim," I told them.

"That's okay. We'll teach you," they offered. "You should come. It'll be fun."

The idea that they were much older than I was should have tipped me off that their intentions were not entirely pure. Against my better judgment, I went with them. I trailed behind them by a few steps and listened while they talked and joked along the way to the water, paying little attention to me. They carried towels, and they all wore bathing suits. I had never seen such an outfit before, but was certainly not going to mention that fact to anyone.

When we arrived at the lake, they told me the water was so shallow that a person could walk from one end to the other. They encouraged me to give it a try, so I did. Step by step, I walked into the green, algae-filled water, with growing confidence in my new "friends." I walked a few steps farther, and without warning, it felt as though the floor of the lake had been pulled out from under me. I could not feel the bottom any longer. I was in trouble, and I panicked.

I did not know what to do, but before I lost all hope, I felt a strength come over me, prompting me to move my hands and remain calm. I paddled for my life and slowly reached the shore. I approached the edge of the lake, and I could see the kids laughing at me as they ran off in the distance. Humiliated, I ran to our room in my soaking wet dress. I was afraid to go out for fear they would take advantage of me again. The experience cultivated a lifelong fear of deep water.

For some reason, I liked to be around mothers with babies. I guess I felt safer around them because they did not trick me or hurt me. One day, walking by myself near a brook, I saw two women talking and a baby in a carriage, crying hysterically. I stopped to ask one of the women if I could push her carriage back and forth along the path to calm her baby. "Oh, yes! That would be nice," said the woman, seeming more interested in her conversation than in her child.

I paced twenty feet or so in either direction. The gentle rocking of the carriage and the sounds of the rushing water from the brook calmed the baby, and she soon stopped crying. After a few times up and down the path, I turned to make my way back toward where the ladies were seated, awkwardly maneuvering the carriage's oversized white rubber wheels, which I found difficult to control. I managed to turn the carriage, and it rolled dangerously close to the brook. I tried, with limited success, to maintain control. I struggled with the carriage, almost arguing with it, over which of us would determine our destination. When one of the carriage wheels caught the edge of the brook's bank, and jerked one of my hands free from the handle bar, I lost my grip on the carriage and called for help. Still holding on with one hand, I did my best to regain command of the carriage as we picked up speed and bounded over the embankment. Again I called for help, but the woman continued talking with her friend; oblivious to my predicament.

The carriage continued into the gully with the baby inside and me skidding and sliding behind. Finally, the carriage tipped sideways and splashed into the water, dragging me along with it. I quickly pulled the baby out and brought it, dripping wet, to the mother. She did not scold me, but I ran home as fast as I could for fear the Gestapo would come looking for me.

Gretchen returned home on a break from boarding school. During one of our brief encounters, she presented me with a picture of her and her friend. Pictures were not so common, so I held it in my possession with great pride; particularly because it came from Heinrich's daughter. I wanted her to like me, and looked forward to every opportunity to chat. During one of our chats, Gretchen told me about a boy, whom she liked, who lived down the road. She handed me an envelope with a letter inside, and told me to go to his house to deliver the letter to him. Happy to help, I dashed off, down the road, to the boy's house with the letter in hand. When I entered the courtyard of the boy's home, I was greeted by two large dogs. I don't know if they ever barked or even growled at me. The mere sight of them scared my legs into immediate motion. I turned and dashed down the road back toward Heinrich's farm, but not before flinging the letter into the boy's courtyard.

I had fun with some of the other German kids on a few occasions. They taught me to cartwheel, swing on the bridge railings, and walk on the beams over the dam. Unfortunately, it was more common for them to belittle me, make fun of me, or take their frustrations out on me. One afternoon, while walking toward Heinrich's house, a twelve- or thirteen-year-old boy caught up to me. "After we win the war, you will be my personal slave," he said.

His statement surprised me so much that I answered without thinking, "I will never be your slave, and you won't win the war."

At that, he punched me so hard in the stomach that I buckled over and fell to the ground. He ran off, and I gasped for air for what seemed like an eternity. Regaining my breath, I walked slowly back to my room. When Mama got home that evening from work, I could not wait to tell her about my encounter. With fear in her eyes, she advised me not to discuss politics, war, or anything controversial with anyone. Otherwise, we could end up in a concentration camp. It was the first time I had heard the term.

We learned many new terms around that time. Bits and pieces about what the Nazis were doing to what they called subversives were surfacing. Following those experiences, a growing fear caused me to avoid German people, especially the children. From that point on, Mama prepared schoolwork for me on a piece of paper, and I spent my days alone in our room, practicing my Polish alphabet.

Fear was a constant factor of everyday life in Germany. We were always fearful. Fearful of what we knew. Fearful of what we didn't know. Fearful of what we saw. Fearful of what we couldn't see. Fearful about what we said and to whom we were speaking. It was a common practice that if someone stood on a street corner to engage another in conversation, they looked over their shoulder to ensure nobody was watching them. Otherwise, they might be accused of conspiracy.

The adults were not able to provide a good example for not being afraid. They were fearful, too. It showed on their faces, and it showed in their general behavior. Everything around us encouraged a sense of fear and apprehension. The frequent searches of our rooms added to the trepidation, the distrust, and the uncertainty. Over time, I watched as even the strongest of the adults were worn down, submitting to it.

Babcia and Dziadzio with their children during happier times. From left to right, the children are Uncle Walter, Aunt Julia, my mother Maria, and Aunt Genevieve.

June 5, 1933: Mama and Tatus's wedding. They are seated in the center, directly behind the children in the first row. Everyone was there except Helena.

Tatus. He had big plans for me.

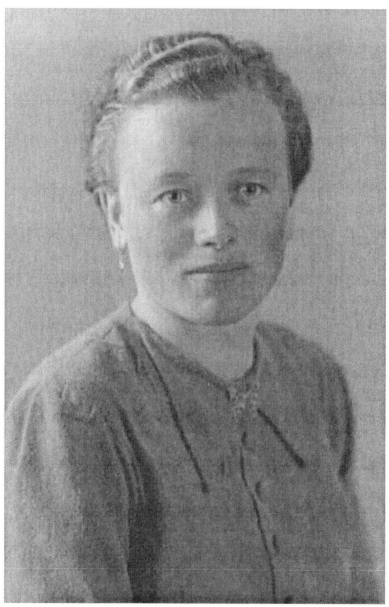

Mama, soon after arriving at the first slave labor camp in Germany. The stress had not yet taken its toll on her innocent, wholesome appearance.

Me at the first slave labor camp with a borrowed teddy bear. This photo was taken shortly after we arrived. We were always hungry, and my stomach growled loudly as I posed for this picture. The shoes were hand-me-downs; two sizes too big.

Aunt Julia and me at the first camp.

In front of Heinrich's fruit garden, 1941. Mama (L), Aunt Julia (R) and me.

Ropcyzce, 1942. With brother, Leon. Finally, I had someone to play with.

My First Holy Communion celebrated in the Wildflecken DP camp, 1946. After the war, the UNRRA provided us with clothes like the suit that Mama wore for my special day. Leon is on my left.

Mama in Wildflecken, 1946. The innocence was gone from her face. By then, she had reached her breaking point.

Stepfather, in his Polish military uniform before we met.

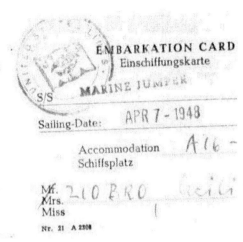

EMBARKATION CARD
Einschiffungskarte

S/S   MARINE JUMPER

Sailing-Date: APR 7 - 1948

Accommodation   A 16 -
Schiffsplatz

Mr.   2(0 BRO   Geili
Mrs.
Miss

Nr. 21 A 2308

My boarding card to America. I made sure to count the smokestacks on the ship.

These pigeons served their country, and then were served ...for dinner. I'm on the right.

New York, 1953. I was nineteen.

CHAPTER 7
BACK AND FORTH

June, 1941. One night, I was awakened by multiple whispering voices, hours before sunrise. As I lay on my straw mattress, I could hear the cautious tone of adults engaged in dialogue. Mama's inquiring voice interacted with a few low monotone voices. Except for a few words, I couldn't understand anything. Although I didn't recognize any of the voices except for Mama's, one name that I heard them say throughout the conversation was "Leon." The next morning, I asked Mama who came to see us so late in the evening, and she told me that they were Polish partisans, part of the Underground. Mama said they gave her information about the war, concentration camps, and what was going on in the world. Over the next few days, I heard the adults quietly recount the stories that were told that evening about "people being terribly mistreated, not being fed," and how we might end up "if we aren't careful." Little did we know how bad it really was.

By 1942, times had gotten increasingly difficult. Even though I spoke German fairly well by then, neither pencils nor paper were available to practice my alphabet. Boredom often frustrated me during those years, and I concocted any number of silly little games to play by myself, to keep the boredom at bay. Winters were particularly long and boring because I did not have warm clothes to go out to play, so I stayed inside.

I couldn't take the boredom any longer. In my light dress and no panties, I braved the snow and cold, one day, to slide down a large hill. I trudged to the top, with snow filling my shoes. From the top of the hill, I got a running start, jumped into the air, and assumed the seated, driving position that whisked me down the hillside, with the wind blowing through my hair. Unfortunately, it didn't work out quite that way. On the contrary, I landed hard into cold, wet snow and jutted forward maybe five feet. Snow filled my dress and surrounded my bare body. Looking around in case someone saw me, I got up and concluded that it was more comfortable to be bored and warm in the room than entertained and freezing outside.

When the German kids were at school and the workers were in the field, the hours of silence sometimes generated a feeling of paranoia. "Who is watching me? Did I just hear something?" I felt like I was the only one on that farm and in the whole world.

I often went to the field to help Mama keep up with the workers, especially when she wasn't well. I wanted a sibling to play with and nagged Mama about it, almost daily. I didn't know she needed a husband for that. One day Mama told me that she was planning to get me a sibling. I was beside myself in excitement. She told me she made arrangements with the stork to bring us a baby.

In the winter of 1942, January, Mama negotiated with Heinrich to let her go to Poland to have the baby. Heinrich agreed and gave us a pass. We packed up our little suitcase and, as was customary, Olga performed a cursory search and then released us. We finished packing, and at the precise moment that we were leaving our room for the train station, we were stopped and searched again. Heinrich and his wife came to our room, unannounced. "Open your suitcase," demanded Heinrich. They rummaged through every little piece of clothing we had. What they were looking for, I don't know, but when they finished, without a word, they left. It was stunning, and yes, frightening.

We went back to Poland on a passenger train. The train stations were always overcrowded with SS and German soldiers. Their presence alone inflicted fear. Thank goodness Mama kept our papers handy and in good condition. That minimized our interaction with them. We came back to Granice and lived with Babcia in her one-room house. There, we learned that, except for the youngest, all of Babcia's children were taken as slave laborers.

Within weeks, on February 4, 1942, Mama gave birth to my brother, and I named him: Leon. He was delivered by a midwife who also served as Leon's godmother. At almost eight years old, I was ecstatic that I finally had a brother to play with and keep me company. For the first few months, however, Mama forbade me to touch him. I could only look at him and watch him while he slept. I also stood by when my mother nursed him. He was a good baby. Perfectly content. He rarely cried.

During our time back in Poland, Mama wrote often to Andrzej. In those days, mail pickup and delivery was a luxury that had not yet come to Granice, so Mama told me to watch Leon while she went to the post office in Ropczyce to drop off her letters.

Mama enrolled me at school in Ropczyce. Finally there was something to take the place of the boredom. I looked forward to most of my classes. I enjoyed learning and being around other children. After a few days, once my shyness wore off, I befriended the girl who sat behind me in religion class. She had blue eyes and medium-length blond hair. She wondered why I hadn't been at school until then. Being quite ashamed of our situation, I told her that I had been in Germany, but gave few details as to why we were there.

"Do you speak German?" she inquired excitedly.

"Yes." I answered with as little information as possible, so as not to reveal what fate had befallen us.

"Well, say something to me in German."

Before I could answer, the priest teaching the class interrupted our conversation, explaining that we should report to detention at the end of the school day for disrupting his lesson. I'm not sure what I was more afraid of, staying after school or the idea that it would be dark before I left school. At that time, Poles were superstitious and particularly afraid of the dark. The strong emphasis on religion often led some to cross the border into a belief in ghosts, demons, and other unknown spirits that were inclined to appear at night. By the end of the long day, everything had worked out fine. Other kids were held after school too, so I had someone to walk with in the dark, and ghosts rarely appear unless you're by yourself –or so I was told.

On one occasion, German soldiers came to my school. They loaded a truck full of Polish children and brought them to a hospital in Germany. Polish parents told of how their children's blood was extracted to give to wounded German soldiers. Some less lucky parents told, in shame, of how their daughters were handed over for the soldiers' pleasures. It wasn't long before Mama kept me home from school altogether.

Mama sowed wheat on the piece of rented land in Granice. It was growing strong and straight with numerous buds all around, until the morning we woke to discover that the crops had been vandalized. Someone cut the green wheat. We wondered if people had cut it for their own use, but ultimately reasoned that it could not have been used for anything, for it was not yet ripe.

The disappointment showed in Mama's face. She looked beaten, worn, and depressed. "All that work for nothing," she sighed. Nothing was ever said publicly, but we strongly suspected my father's relatives. They antagonized Mama and Babcia to "return the Ziobrowka to the rightful owners." Because my father was gone, they argued that the land belonged to them. The arguments were infrequent, but the annoyance lingered as Mama or Babcia invariably came across a member of the Ziobro family on the road or in town. Whatever the occasion, it presented an opportunity to express ill feelings over the property.

Living with Babcia was not easy. She and Mama quarreled frequently. Arguments over "what is yours and what is mine" were most common. "I've told you before," Babcia proclaimed, "Your cow is to be kept on the Ziobrowka! Keep her *off* my property!"

A few weeks later, it was Mama's turn to assert herself, "Mama, will you please stop milking my cow! We've been over this many times. I have two children. They need my cow's milk."

One morning, Babcia grew furious. "I take you into my home to provide a roof over the head of you and two children, and you won't let me share your cow's milk, but you have no problem letting your cow graze on my property?" she accused.

"My cow doesn't graze on your property!"

"Oh, she doesn't? You think I don't know what goes on at my house when I go into town?" she responded with a judicious glare. Mama was clearly unaware that her little sister Helena was recruited as an unknowing informant each time Babcia left the property.

"Your children are grown," fired back Mama, "and they can work to support themselves and the rest of the family. My children are young, and they need all of the nourishment they can get."

The argument escalated until Babcia got so angry that she marched over to the stable, removed the rope from the cow, and pointed toward the door. "So this is how you speak to your mother? Okay! Keep your cow, but get out of my house! Get out!" she shrieked and opened the door.

The tension in the household had been growing for some time, and Mama had been looking around for another place to live. Looking outside, she paused for a split second, clearly weighing whether a cold snowy day was the best time to take a stand. But Mama had some of her mother's stubbornness in her, so she quickly snapped back into character. She gathered our few belongings, picked up infant Leon who was but a few weeks old, and grabbed the cow's rope from her mother's hand. She called for me to come. I buttoned up my coat as quickly as I could, and we headed out the door.

The cold air penetrated our coats and hats, numbing our bodies to the bone. We trudged through the light snow as it accumulated. The cow slipped and slid as we made our way down the road. Under different circumstances, it would have been almost comical to watch us pulling a cow that appeared to be on roller skates. The sun rose higher in the sky behind the dark clouds. We walked northeast for a few miles to the next village, Chechly, where Mama had heard that there was a place for rent.

We arrived at an old, spooky house on the main road and were let into the home by a neighbor. We hurried inside to get out of the cold. It was a one-room house with a straw roof, dirt floor, and storage closets on one wall. Interestingly enough, we never opened those closets. We didn't have anything to store. The house had no bathroom, no water facilities, or heat. The cow stayed in the same room with us. The whole house smelled of manure, but the cow's warm body was a creative way to take the bite off the dry, winter air. The house was still cold, but it sure beat being outside in the snow.

By then I had outgrown my clothes. Mama made me a dress from a plaid tablecloth. Firewood was scarce, because the ground was usually covered with snow and clear of fallen trees. Without wood to make a fire in the stove to warm the water, we did not bathe often. Instead we pulled water from a nearby well and rubbed the dirt off with a damp towel. Because we had no heat, if it wasn't raining or snowing, we hung our clothes to dry outside in the evening breeze. Otherwise, we hung them inside. In the morning, when we went to put our clothes on again, the first question of the day was whether they had dried completely. Often they had not, and we started the day wearing cold, damp clothing.

Babcia made life especially miserable for my mother during that time. Among other things, she mailed Mama's pictures to us with Mama's eyes peeled out. She forbade Mama's sisters and brothers to visit. Babcia banished us. Regardless, Aunt Genevieve did stop by from time to time, under the strict understanding that the visits were never to be mentioned. The list of hurtful things she did was long. *Grandma Dearest* could have been a bestseller.

We had lived in that spooky house for a few weeks, when in the middle of the night someone knocked on the door. We were scared and thought it might be the Gestapo. Mama reluctantly opened the door to find a couple with a child in their arms. They asked if Mama would consider putting them up for the night. Mama let them in and asked them to follow her to the closet, where they spent barely a few hours. They left early in the morning, while it was still dark. Mama later told me that they were Jews running away from Hitler and headed for Russia. They asked Mama if they could buy her passport, but she was afraid to sell it. The next morning I noticed a German soldier peeking over a snow bank with his gun. How lucky we were, I thought, that we didn't get caught harboring those poor souls.

Conditions in Poland got to be nearly unlivable. Hitler was slowly choking the life out of everyone and everything there. We were starving, and so was our primary source of sustenance, the cow. Without adequate nourishment, the cow stopped giving milk. Aside from our spooky rented house Poland had, quite literally, nothing to offer us. After weeks of misery, I coaxed Mama to return to the farm, as she promised Heinrich. At least there, we could get bread and soup and possibly steal something to survive. "If we don't go back," I pleaded, "they might come looking for us, and put us in one of those concentration camps."

Toward the end of 1942, when Leon was about seven or eight months old, Mama decided to go back to Heinrich's farm. I was old enough to care for Leon, and Mama felt comfortable knowing that the baby would not be cared for by strangers if we went back. My uncle, John Ziobro, one of the few who chose not to involve himself in the squabble over the Ziobrowka land, brought us to the train station on a horse and buggy. Sheepishly, Babcia and Mama made up, realizing that under those dire circumstances, it was no time to hold grudges. Mama gave our cow and land to Babcia and said a good-bye for what might be the last time.

On the train back to Germany, we sat quietly. I heard the conductor at the other end of the car talking to passengers and checking tickets. On the bench next to us sat a woman who made it clear to anyone who listened that she was being shipped to a forced labor camp. Most listened politely, but said little. My mother sat closest to her, and I sat next to Mama near the aisle. The woman sat by the window, at arm's length from the door.

She spoke in a firm tone to a few others on the train as it chugged along at about sixty miles per hour. She solemnly explained that she would not be held against her will. One way or another, she was going to get out of her predicament. The train continued to zip along. Although she stopped talking at one point, I could see that she continued to ruminate on how to get out of her situation, and then, in a methodical manner, she leaned forward and extended her hand toward the door latch. She slowly lifted the handle and pushed the train door open. Before she could steady herself, a strong gust of wind flung the door open, pulling her out of the railcar and sending her to an almost certain death. The momentum almost pulled Mama with her. It happened so quickly that nobody said a single word. Luckily Mama held on to a neighboring passenger, who helped her from being pulled out as well. A man got up from his seat and matter-of-factly closed the door. Whether the woman survived the fall or not, one way or another, she succeeded in escaping her captors. Still, not a word was spoken and the train continued toward Germany.

CHAPTER 8
SURVIVING ON FAITH

When we arrived back at the farm, we found the camp in much the same condition as when we left. Most, if not all, of the same people were there. Mama instructed me to begin calling Andrzej Tatus, which I conveniently forgot to do most of the time. Andrzej stayed with us in a bigger room in the same house, one where we had stayed before. Aunt Julia stayed with us, too. It seemed that although we were separated from time to time, Aunt Julia was often in our company. Because I seemed to "forget," Mama and Andrzej frequently reminded me to address Andrzej as Tatus. Sometimes I outright refused, and he threatened me. Aunt Julia told Andrzej that he should not strike me because I was not his child. That worked.

Andrzej was from Torun, Poland. He was a forest ranger before the war. He had a wife and two daughters. The Russians shipped them to Siberia, he told us. I never heard him talk about his family. I only knew what my mother told me about them. He and Mama worked from early morning to late at night, and I took care of little Leon. Mama resumed most of the same duties as she held before we left, which included milking the cows. Each time Mama milked a cow, I came to her with a white cup and, when nobody was looking, she filled it with fresh milk for Leon and me to drink. Not long after starting this practice, I noticed a man, about thirty feet away, ducking down behind the cows at the other end of the stable. He looked to be in his twenties, slim with dark hair. I saw him there every day. After a few days, I asked Mama what he was doing. "He's German," she explained, "but he doesn't want to fight in the war, so he hides here, between the cows, scrounging whatever food he can get his hands on."

From time to time we came across German people willing to help us. A German family once lent us a sewing machine so Mama could make clothes for us after work. The next day, they came and took it back, saying that they would get in trouble with the German government. Another German woman, who rented a room on Heinrich's farm, was unusually civil toward me. She talked sweetly and gently to me. She never did anything in particular for me. I was just grateful for her kindness. I liked her.

A German family gave us a baby carriage that we used more for a carnival ride than its intended purpose. When Mama left for work, I pulled out the carriage, pushed it up a little hill, piled myself in with Leon, and off we went, those big white rubber wheels bounding down the hillside. Whenever we hit a rut or a stone along the way, the carriage tipped over. We tumbled out, and our flailing bodies rolled down the rest of the hill. We laughed and giggled the whole way down. At least I laughed and giggled. Leon usually wound up with bumps and scratches all over his body. When Mama asked me why Leon was bruised so often, I issued my prepared reply. "Well, you know how he climbs on things all the time and falls. He's very clumsy." That fib worked only until Leon grew old enough to talk. He eventually spilled the beans, and my carnival ride closed.

One day my mother told me that the German woman who lived above the stable had a baby, and that I should go see what the stork had brought. When I went up the stairs to her room, I saw the mother holding the baby. I looked carefully at the baby's red face and hands, but said nothing to the woman, so as not to wake the sleeping baby. The woman nodded to me, and I nodded back. I quietly stepped down the stairs and reported back to my mother. She asked, "Did you see the baby?"

"Yes," I said, "but I don't think the stork brought him. The baby is all red. I think the baby was in her stomach. She used to be fat, and now she's skinny."

Mama smiled but said nothing.

In the beginning, Heinrich gave us food to eat. Eventually he gave us food stamps to buy bread, sugar, lard, and flour to make dumplings. His farm continued to provide potatoes. Mama sent me to do the shopping at the mercantile in the next village. After a long walk, I arrived at the store. I pulled open the front door and was greeted by the smell of all sorts of delicious foods: bacon, sausage, vegetables, and so many other things we could never afford. A few people stood in line at the counter, while others milled around. Everyone stared at my raggedy clothes that were clearly too small for me. Some were more obvious than others in the way they stared. I tried not to notice. Even though only the grownups were required to wear the "P" on their shirts, identifying them as forced laborers, my tattered clothes and worn shoes told everyone who I was. I was eight and a half years old and uncomfortable in that environment. When I got to the front of the line, I handed the clerk the food stamps and, in German, told him what I needed: bread, flour, and sugar.

When I arrived home, I had to peel and boil the potatoes, so that when Mama got back from the fields she had something to eat. It was difficult for a kid my age. To start boiling the potatoes, I had to make a fire in the stove. I collected twigs, gathered from the woods and stored in a corner near the washroom. I grabbed a few logs from outside the house and placed them on top of the twigs. With the box of wooden matches on the shelf, I lit a flame and fanned it until it spread. When the fire got hot enough, I filled our only pot with water and placed it on the cinder stove.

The food stamps were no more plentiful than the food itself. We ran out of both frequently, so we had to steal. At times I followed the harvest machine in the fields and collected the remnants that fell behind. In the fall, I picked the wheat that fell from the processing machines used by the laborers each day. I did my best to collect it by hand and put it in a bag. I had a great deal of time on my hands, because I had no friends to play with and I did not go to school.

Even though it might take me a whole day to extract a little wheat, it didn't matter. I had nothing else to do.

Gathering wheat became an everyday activity for me. At whatever time of day I gathered the wheat, I was sure to stay out there until the workers passed by me on their way back from the fields. As they passed me, I carefully eavesdropped on their conversations. I overheard them say that we only had so many days to pick before the first frost came. I knew that gave me a small window of time to gather whatever I could. In a few days, after the workers picked the fields clean, the land would be turned over for the next crop, and my opportunity would pass me by, so I picked faster. I was like a squirrel, storing nuts before the winter, and it helped my family survive. I gathered wheat until I had enough to take one or two pounds to the flour mill. On each trip, the owner of the mill gave me flour for our family in exchange for the wheat I gave him.

While walking home after each trip, I wondered if what I did was a sin. I never came to a moral resolution for taking the wheat. I knew only that we needed to eat somehow, so I quietly continued the process throughout our time at the farm. If adults had tried to do what I did, they would have been arrested. In retrospect, even though my tattered clothing gave me away as a forced laborer, the fact that I was a child with blond hair, who spoke German reasonably well allowed me to get away with more than I otherwise should have. I was too big to get into the chicken coop, so I couldn't pilfer any more eggs. The fruit trees on the property, however, were an easy target, and I exploited them whenever the opportunity arose. I had diarrhea all the time, but didn't know why.

After getting disbanded and beaten by the Gestapo for gathering, we devised a different plan for getting together. On Sundays, our day of rest, two or three of us left our rooms for "a walk into the woods." After a while, a few more left for a walk into the woods, and then a few more. And then a few more. We all walked deep into the woods, and met at a predetermined location, far from the farm, far from the guards. It was our refuge, our place to relax. We sang and danced. We told stories and counted all the planes going by. I wanted to believe they were American planes, but I could only hope. We could rarely tell for sure.

We talked about the war and how people came to this farm from their place of birth. We talked about what we were going to do after the war ended. Mama always broadcast how she planned to return to America. Despite countless warnings, she took great pride in telling her fellow prisoners that she was an American, "and that there's no way they're sending me back to Poland after the war. My children and I are going to America."

Our meetings in the forest always consisted of a handful of activities, each occurring in specific order. We talked for a little while, then sang, and then danced. Next, someone told a story or two. Every so often, from off in the distance, someone would hear a low humming sound. "Listen," they'd whisper, and everyone would freeze. We looked up at the sky to count the planes as they flew over our heads and past the forest trees. Because the partisans kept us reasonably well informed, we felt confident that the planes were, in fact, American. Still, we stared and squinted when they drew near, hoping to make out the insignia of the American flag on their wings as they zoomed by. They were high in the air, and while we fixed our gaze on them from such a long distance, they appeared to move closer and closer to the treetops as they traversed the sky overhead.

The partisans told us the Americans were beginning to bomb factories, bridges, and big cities. Thankfully they stayed away from the farms and open fields where we were. Nonetheless, taking no chances, we studied the bellies of the planes and the sky beneath them, in case someone spotted a falling bomb. We had all learned back in Poland what it was like to be under fire during an aerial attack. If someone saw something suspicious, we were prepared to scatter.

One time while our group of laborers and family members were out in the woods, a big storm surprised us. Dark clouds rolled in, quickly followed by lightning and thunder. I thought the sky was going to fall on us. Mama told me to take Leon and go back to our room. I reluctantly headed back, but was petrified of the storm, and especially the thunder. I carried Leon on my back for the long walk and cried all the way home. Out of breath and with tears still flowing down my cheeks, I reached a café and stopped there to rest. I panned the room and saw a large group of jovial townspeople, happily eating and drinking. The walls were off-white, and the room was filled with tables and chairs. Leon and I stood under an awning, waiting for the rain to stop, and a man came over to us. He noticed that I was crying, so he leaned over and handed me a glass of dark beer. I had never tasted beer before. Thirsty and tired, I reached for it and drank until the unique taste caught my attention. I paused for a minute, looked at the glass, and concluded that I liked it. *"Danke,"* I said with a nod and then licked the froth from my upper lip. After my brother and I rested for a while, he and I continued to our quarters, and the storm subsided.

CHAPTER 9
EVEN THEIR ANIMALS!

By the end of 1943, Mama was not well. She convinced Heinrich to let her go to a place where the work was less demanding. Heinrich agreed, and gave us a pass to move to a smaller farm, not far from our current location. Mama, Andrzej, Leon, and I lived there in a small room above a stable.

At our new location, Mama and Andrzej worked from morning to late at night, and I continued to take care of little Leon. A trip to the outhouse marked the opening act for each day. That performance proved insignificant until the seasons changed and the temperature dropped through the autumn into winter. Daylight hours dwindled into December, and we dragged our exhausted bodies through the darkness, across the courtyard, over to the outhouse, in the frigid morning air. Those morning excursions prompted a bit of creativity. Mama put a pot near the window. We urinated into the pot, lifted the window, and dumped out the contents. That plan worked fine until the summer came, when the heat and humidity magnified the putrid smell of urine, creeping into our room from outside. So much for an "indoor toilet."

We were fed potato puree topped with bacon fat, with no bacon to be seen. Although the meals were not haute cuisine, I still looked forward to whatever food they offered.

When I turned ten on June 1, 1944, the farmer told me I would be treated as an adult. I took pride in his declaration, until Mama provided the sobering translation. As she put it, "If you work, then you can eat."

My new responsibilities included taking care of the chickens, geese, ducks, and cows, in addition to little Leon. My morning routine started around dawn with the other "adults." I went to the stable and took each cow off its chain and brought them to pasture. The cows, maybe four or five of them, had schlepped themselves over to the meadow so often that they knew the way as well as I did.

They followed me out to the fields. I left them there, within the boundaries of the wire fence that surrounded the pasture. I walked back to the stable, scraped out the manure, and laid fresh straw for the cows. To put the manure on the wagon, I used a pitch fork and levered it over the side rail. When the wagon was full, I steered it over to the manure pile and tipped the contents of the wagon onto the pile. After laying the new straw, I went back to the stable to feed the chickens, geese, and ducks. In the corner of the stable was a forty- or fifty-pound burlap bag of feed. Each morning I dug into it with an old plate and spread the feed around the dirt courtyard grounds.

I also helped the farmer's wife, Leyna, pick fruit for canning. Leyna had a medium build, a grandmotherly figure who always wore a babushka. She was in her fifties, I'd say. We picked gooseberries, currants, and cherries all growing in their own separate area of her garden. Each berry patch covered about a square yard or so. We picked whatever was ripe at that time of the year. One day Leyna prepared a basket of food for me to bring to the workers. When I arrived, the workers told me to put the lunch on a particular patch of grass. I did, and went running back to the farm.

When the workers returned home in the evening, they said they never saw the lunch. Furthermore, when they went to find the basket of food, it wasn't there. I assumed a hungry person, hiding in the woods, took it. "Maybe American soldiers or partisans," Mama and Andrzej supposed. We knew it couldn't have been wild animals who took the food, because neither the plate nor a single morsel of food was left on the ground. As much as I knew Leyna liked me, I knew not to mention that partisans were roaming the area. I was happy she liked me, but even at ten years old, I quickly learned whose side I was on.

In addition to the multiple fruit trees and fertile farm fields, the farmer cultivated honey from a small collection of hives on the property. When the farmer headed to the field with the workers one morning, he turned back in my direction on his way past the bee hives. "If you ever see a swarm of honey bees leaving their hive, grab a hose and douse them with water, so they return to the hive." I kept a distant eye on the hives over the next few days. When I discovered a swarm of bees departing the hive as a group, I put his instructions into practice ... well, almost. I couldn't find a hose. Instead, I went back to the well and filled a pail almost to the top with water. I hobbled back to the hive. About a quarter of the water had spilled over the edges, but I still had plenty left. With a running start, I heaved the pail of water at the hive. My momentum carried me less than a foot from the swarming bees. My reward for completing my task was the throbbing pain and swelling of a large bee's stinger lodged in my cheek. In a frenzied panic, I pulled at the stinger to relieve the four-alarm fire on my skin, and managed to dislodge it. The experience served as a reminder to investigate better ways for "dousing a swarm of bees." I have to say that, despite the pain, I found it interesting to learn how the farmer extracted honey.

He returned from the fields at the end of the day, and saw my swollen, red cheek. Ashamed, I turned away from him. He walked over to the bee hive and pulled out one of the honeycomb forms used to extract the honey. He studied it to make sure that there wasn't a stray bee hiding in the form, and then called me over. Before cleaning the form, he handed it to me and let me lick the fresh, golden honey dripping from the wooden frame. The farmer smiled at me, and placed the honeycomb form back in its place.

I got up one bright, warm morning as usual and prepared to do my chores. I brought the cows out to pasture, cleaned the barn, removed the manure, and put fresh straw down for the cows. I picked up the bag of feed for the chickens and geese that rested against the wall near the barn door. As I spread the feed around, I saw a mother goose run toward me. I suppose I came too close to her chicks. She jumped on my shoulders and pecked my head.

Hard as I tried, I could not get her off my shoulders. I suppose I looked funny running around the courtyard with a goose flapping her wings above me. We created quite a commotion. She hovered over my tiny body like a helicopter, with her wings spread. No sooner did I get her off me, like a magnet, she jumped right back on top of my shoulders and continued her work on the top of my head. Finally I grabbed her by the neck, swung her around, and threw her as far away as I could, before racing to the stable. Out of breath, I looked up to see the farmer's fourteen-year-old son standing at the door, doubled over in side-splitting laughter. A member of the German youth group, he was visiting his family on a break from the boarding school where he practiced to become a proud Nazi soldier.

Leon, on the other hand, had a more violent encounter with a rooster who jumped on top of his tiny head and almost pecked his eyes out. The rooster pecked a hole on his forehead, right between his eyes, and left Leon bleeding profusely. He was two years old. I thought, *"My goodness, not only are the adults and kids mean, but so are their animals."*

The following day, before sunset, I headed out to bring the five or six cows back from pasture. I pushed and prodded them toward the barn, but noticed that one cow was not interested in cooperating. She was clearly agitated. It only took a few more prods and pushes before her agitation turned to anger. She snorted and stammered wildly with her gaze now fixed on a target: me.

It's sort of curious how, as a young girl, you don't need any particular experience or knowledge to tell you that it's time to go. With my eyes still watching the cow's every move, I turned and slowly inched my way toward the post and wire fence. The animal's anger grew, and my pace accelerated. She started toward me with her head down, her furrowed brow pointed in my direction. I opened up into an all-out sprint, hoping there was enough distance between us to save my behind (literally). I had no more chances to look back. I would either make it to the other side of the fence safely or not.

With each step, I could hear the thunder of hooves. She was getting closer. The ground rumbled beneath my feet. *"She has me,"* I thought. Like a kid on a playground, I slid under the fence and scrambled to the other side. I could feel her breath on my legs as I pulled them barely out of reach. I rolled over. The cow stared at me, let out an abrupt snort, and then confidently strutted away. Heaving for air with sweat dripping from my body, I lay behind the safety of the fence, comforted by the wet, soft ground. I rested there for a long while to regain my composure. After my breaths became more measured and I stopped shaking from the rush of adrenaline, I relaxed, noticing how good the cold, wet grass felt. I lay there even longer, looking up at the clouds, listening to the birds. That day, someone else brought the cows in.

Weeks after that incident, Tante Leyna (Aunt Leyna, which is how she now wanted me to address her) called me to come help her pick cherries from the trees in the garden. I often accompanied Tante Leyna when she picked fruit from the trees. I enjoyed climbing up the ladder and onto the branches. Tante Leyna dragged the ladder out of the barn and propped it up against the trunk of a tree. Handing me a pail, she motioned for me to start climbing, while she steadied the ladder below. "Pick only the ripe ones," she said in German.

Tante Leyna encouraged me. She sometimes told me what a hard worker I was, which always made me feel good. This time, however, I felt a growing pain in my back, so my pace was slower than usual. I resumed my climb and shrugged off the pain. While I pulled the cherries off the branches, the pain grew sharper. I stretched to reach the cherries with one hand and hold on to the ladder with the other, but it seemed as though the energy were being sucked out of my body. My legs struggled to support my body, and I began to shake. I sat for a minute on the top rung of the ladder and then went back to picking. I picked a few cherries and then rested again to regain my strength. I picked a few more and rested a little longer. Tante

Leyna soon noticed that I spent more time resting than picking, but from her vantage point she couldn't exactly see what was happening up there. Impatient and confused, she called for me to pick up the pace. "Stop eating the cherries! You're eating more than you're sending down!"

I wasn't eating cherries, though, and by then I was drained of energy. She saw that something wasn't right, but still wasn't sure whether I was truly in pain. She ordered me to get down from the ladder. We switched places. Tante Leyna climbed the ladder and proceeded to fill the bucket. As she picked the cherries, she looked back down to the bottom of the ladder to ensure I was in proper position to catch the bucket when it came down. Instead, she saw me lying on the ground. Still puzzled, she impatiently continued picking, summoning me to "get up" when her bucket was full.

She continued to pass the cherries to me, and I did my best to catch the bucket each time it came down. Tante Leyna's demeanor changed back and forth between concern and anger, as she still could not be sure whether I was sick, tired, or faking. When it came time to pick up and bring everything inside, she backed her way down the ladder and said, "Well, I guess that's all we'll have time for today. Let's go inside, Cecylia."

I could not get up. "Get up," she insisted. When she realized I was not pretending, she lifted me up under my armpits and dragged me into the house. When Mama got back from the field, it was too late to go to the doctor. We had to wait until morning. I moaned and cried all through the sleepless night.

In the morning, the farmer boss lifted me from the floor, carried me to his horse and buggy, and drove Mama and me to the next village to see the doctor. While he drove, I lay there on a bed of straw, screaming in pain each time the carriage hit a bump in the road.

Mama held me up and dragged me into the doctor's office, because I couldn't stand on my own. The farmer sat in the wagon and waited. We awkwardly entered the office, with Mama trying to hold me and push the door open. The doctor's office was full of adults and children of all ages. We had to stand in line. I could hear the German kids in the waiting room, laughing at me. One of them said, "Look at the Polish swine. She can't even stand up."

Our turn finally came. The doctor examined me; touching my back, my legs, and checking my heart and lungs. He spoke with Mama and gave me some medication. I had an inflammation of the kidneys, he said. He suspected they got infected during my long rest on the cold, wet grass following my race with the cow.

I lay on my back for three months. Tante Leyna often came up to our quarters and brought me cherries and other fresh fruit to eat, along with her homemade preserves. Sick with fever, I could not eat any of it. Once she realized how sick I was, she could not do enough for me. Every day, from then on, she visited me while Mama worked in the fields. She talked to me and told me she wanted to adopt me.

CHAPTER 10
WE'RE POLISH! WE'RE POLISH!

In the autumn of 1944, I was back on my feet again. I was still quite weak but clearly recovering from the kidney infection. By then we saw the suffering of wounded German soldiers and the war's impact on the German families where we lived.

Tante Leyna had two sons. We knew that one of them served in the military, and the other, a fourteen-year-old, was a member of a German youth group. In the early fall, Tante Leyna's eldest son returned from the German front missing his left arm. With the casualties of war in our midst, merely a matter of weeks passed before the war itself came right to our doorstep.

The farm where we stayed stood at the top of a hill. It was part of a community of small farms, single-family homes, and a cemetery that all sat neatly nestled in a clearing surrounded by the densely packed forest. I often helped Tante Leyna bring flowers to the cemetery and maintain the grounds around her deceased relatives. From the farm, we walked along a dirt road through the woods and down the hill to the train station whenever a trip into town was required. When we walked toward the train station, we usually heard the blades buzzing from the nearby sawmill, which also served as a factory for making wooden rifle butts in support of the Nazi effort. Depending on which way the wind blew, we could sometimes smell the tang of freshly cut lumber. After the Allies pushed east into Germany, when we walked down the hill, the unpleasant odor of sulfur from frequent artillery fire in the distance overshadowed the once-pleasant aroma.

Mama's health was deteriorating quickly, so she asked the farmer to give us permission to work in the sawmill where the workload was lighter. The harvest before the winter had already been picked, so the farmer agreed. The Allies were, by that time, bombing bridges, factories, and train stations. For the first time, we saw and heard the sounds of the war directly upon us. The question I didn't think to ask myself was whether we would be liberated before Mama's condition worsened to the point that the Nazis considered her more of a liability than an asset. I can only imagine what would have happened to us then.

When we arrived at the small mill, we saw stacks of gun butts, logs, and lumber neatly piled in the yard, with sawdust blanketing the grounds. Inside the adjacent factory, Mama and Andrzej were instructed as to how the lumber should be taken into the factory and how it was to be manufactured into a finished product. "You are not allowed in the sawmill or the factory," Mama told me. "The machines here are very dangerous and a child would be in the way or get hurt." I was responsible for taking care of Leon, instead. Mama, Andrzej, Leon, and I were assigned a small sleeping room above the factory. There we met other Polish people with whom we shared stories at the end of the day. We learned the Nazis shipped women with children to this location who were captured during the Uprising. The Warsaw (Ghetto) Uprising was a loosely organized attempt to thwart the Nazi effort to transport huge numbers of Polish Jews from their ghetto prisons to extermination camps. As word spread throughout the region of the Nazi plan, an insurgency grew, with small militias joining the fight to free these poor souls. Over a period of months, the Nazis regained control, leaving Warsaw in ashes and much Polish and Jewish blood spilled on its streets. The survivors who joined us at the factory considered themselves lucky. The stories they told of death, torture, concentration camps, and inhumane living conditions were horrifying.

When I wasn't watching Leon, I spent my days exploring my new surroundings, either on my own or when running errands for Mama. The region was rich in natural and manmade beauty. The area had a number of dams, from which German engineers had developed a series of lakes. To pass the time, I sometimes strolled the paths that meandered through and around the forest trees until I reached the nearest dam. I made my way around to the right side of the dam, and carefully stepped along the catwalk at the top of a tall retaining wall against the adjacent dam, almost like a gymnast on a balance beam. When I reached the dam, I stopped, usually for a minute or two. I'd roam around, throw a rock in the water, and then make my way home.

One thing I hated to do was to take the train into town. Every few days, Mama sent me to get pasteurized milk for Leon. In those days, although most everyone in the countryside drank raw milk from the cow, young children were fed this specially processed milk to guard against disease.

For every trip to town, I followed the same procedure. The train pulled into the station. I jumped off the platform and headed for the mercantile. In the beginning, I couldn't read, so I humbly asked for help from an adult to make sure I got off the train at the right stop. Eventually, I grew familiar with my surroundings and managed to find my way on my own. On my first trip, I patiently waited my turn in line. When I got to the counter at the front of the line, the few coins I held so tightly on the train were warm with the moisture from my sweaty palm. I reached up over the counter and handed them to the clerk in exchange for a big, heavy, metal milk container. Now came the tough part. The container was too heavy for me to lift, so I dragged, pulled, and pushed it all the way back to the station, hoisted it up onto the platform (with a little help from the conductor, if I was lucky), and then rode with it back to our train stop.

When the train stopped and everyone got off, they all went the other way, which left just the container and me. The process was bearable in the summer, but in the fall and winter, when it got dark early, I was petrified to lug that thing through the woods all by myself. On those nighttime journeys, I could have easily been shot by a German sentry or an overzealous allied partisan, but other things worried me much more. I had to think of something to keep the ghosts and bears away. All the way home, I cried and screamed as loudly as I could. It worked. Not a single bear or ghost ever got me. Still, I always arrived back at the house trembling and soaked with perspiration and tears, but thoroughly relieved.

In December 1944 through the beginning of 1945, workers spent more time under the factory hiding from the blasts of American artillery than they spent working. Day and night, explosions shook the ground beneath us, and we felt certain we would get hit eventually. We gained up-close knowledge of what war sounded like.

The days passed, and the little food that was available dwindled to nothing. When our hunger became too much to bear, we went into the woods to lick the sap as it oozed from the trees. It did little to satisfy our hunger, but it helped loosen the grip of starvation that was taking hold. As luck would have it, the factory owner was bitten by his dog, so he shot it. The male workers cleaned and butchered it, making a soup for us to eat. All the men ate it with great delight, while the women and children looked on in disgust, unable even to touch their lips to it. After the meal, the women made a point to tease the men, barking at them whenever they wanted the mens' attention.

From the direction where the planes came and went, and especially from the strategic progression of bombing, it was clear to us that the American forces were drawing closer. The bombings grew louder and more intense, and the factory owner told us we were free to leave. He encouraged—almost urged—us to go, a subtle hint that he didn't want to be caught by American troops holding forced laborers. We didn't ask questions. We quickly gathered our things, met our fellow Poles in the courtyard, and agreed to head into the woods.

A light drizzle was falling when we left. We walked through the forest, and the dense tree branches shielded us from what became a steady rain. We stopped at nowhere in particular. Some of the adults put branches on the ground to shield us from the mud and puddles that were soaking into our shoes. We were all hungry. The starvation began to affect our reasoning, but we persevered, hoping, praying, believing that the end of our struggle was closer than it ever had been. One of the adults tore the bark away from the tree trunks. He scraped off the sweet cambium layer between the wood and the bark, and ate it. The rest of us did the same. The rain continued. Water slowly dripped from the branches above. Placing more branches on the ground, we bedded down on the cold April ground to get some rest for the evening.

Throughout the night, except for a few cat naps, we didn't sleep at all. We had nowhere to go and had no information to guide us in one direction or another. A growing sense of danger permeated the air, and our anxiety peaked. We could not be sure who we might come across in the woods, a German soldier, an American soldier; either way, we could get shot. The adults sat up most of the night to keep watch. When morning came, Mama and some others walked to a nearby farm and begged the farmer to take us in, but he said, "I can't take you in, but you shouldn't stay out in the forest. You could get killed in these woods. Partisans, German soldiers, and American artillery are all around. Go back where you came from! You're not safe out here. Go back! They have to take you back!"

We eventually made our way back to the factory. On the night we returned to our quarters, we saw close to one hundred fully geared German soldiers laid out on the main floor, settling in for the night. The soldiers were young, some as young as sixteen years old. Some of the adults in our group advised us not to say a word to them. We whispered among ourselves, but we had no interaction with the soldiers of any kind. As they prepared to bed down, they looked at us and we looked at them. They kept their distance, and so did we. Awkwardly making our way around them, we went up to our quarters and slept for the night.

Once we got settled, one of the men leaned over to Mama and whispered, in a barely audible voice, "You know, there's a real possibility that American soldiers heading this way might be ambushed right here at this factory. The partisans have told us that the Americans are close by. I just don't know how close they are. It could happen, and we'd be right in the middle of it." Mama looked at him but said nothing. The look in her eyes said everything that needed to be said. The thought of a surprise attack breaking out in front of our eyes surely meant the end of us all.

Morning came. When I awoke, I was surprised to find that the German soldiers had all gone. We were all relieved. During those days, we had little food and water, but the smell of sulfur was plentiful. There were about eight or ten of us, some Polish, some Russian. Two of them were single mothers with children about my age. I had someone to play with then, which helped break up the boredom. Aside from Andrzej, Mama, and little Leon, the names and faces of the people who were with us under that factory are blurred in my mind.

These people were faceless and nameless by design. After years in the camps, we learned to trust few people. We never knew who might turn us in for taking a piece of bread or talking out of turn, even those we thought were "our own." As a result, we never got close to anyone or said much to anyone, even in our own group, except for purposes of survival or to gain consensus of what to do next.

For roughly a week, we heard bombings almost daily; usually in the late afternoon and into the evening. During those days, we felt unsafe in our usual quarters of the building, so we moved to the unfinished wooden base on which the now-abandoned factory stood. It was an area of about twenty square feet. The ground was uneven, so it limited the area where we could walk. The bare studs were covered on the exterior of the building by wooden planks in some areas, which kept us mostly hidden from view. Other areas were simply shielded by uneven dirt piled up against the side of the factory.

While we could only hear the planes overhead, the gaps in the planks allowed us to peek out through the walls in case ground troops were visible. When the sound of artillery subsided, we'd come up from our hiding place and assess what little we could of the situation. Although we were terribly hungry, there always seemed to be a piece of bread around, but not much more. During those few days, I kept a close watch over Leon as we wandered about, not far from the factory. Surrounded by rats and living in filth while planes bombed the nearby train station, we were surely resting in the palm of the Lord's hand. Not one bomb fell on us. By that time, we had lost our freedom and our dignity, but our spirit could not be broken. We still had hope, our will to live, and above all, our faith in God.

One spring morning in mid April, we awoke and noticed that the bombing had stopped. A little before noon, we heard activity outside: machinery, tanks, and trucks. We heard talking and the cadenced march of soldiers. The sounds were too muffled to clearly distinguish, and we were too afraid to reveal ourselves or our hiding place, so we stayed put. Finally a few of the adults, including Andrzej, peeked through the gaps in the planks to see what was happening. They saw a single American soldier heading toward us, unaware of our hiding place or that we were even there. Andrzej motioned for all of us to stay still and be quiet.

The soldier drew closer. Our hearts pounded in unison. Finally, from our dark dungeon, we saw him duck into our hideout through a small opening in the wall. Like a tiger, he carefully stepped into the alcove, peering side to side with his head low. He headed toward us with machine gun in hand, and we got a clearer view of him. He was fully armed, with a string of ammunition draped over his shoulders across the back of his neck, and a belt bursting with grenades. Although he still hadn't seen us, his machine gun was pointed in our direction. He was clean shaven, with a razor-thin, waxed mustache that curled up on the ends.

"We're Polish! We're Polish!" we cried. Startled, he raised his gun into position. The sudden spike in tension electrified the room like a lightning bolt. We daringly moved toward him with cautious optimism, holding our hands high in the air. As elated as we were to see him, his intense focus and darting eyes kept us on edge. Despite a language barrier, we needed to be clear about our intentions and avoid any misunderstanding. He took another step closer. He must have noticed our tattered clothes. He surveyed the markings on some of our bodies and clothing, and the expressions on all of our faces. He lowered his gun and, in a split second, turned our hopes and dreams into reality.

That American soldier looked like an angel from heaven to me. I could not take my eyes off him. Until that point in my life, I had never seen anyone so clean and handsome or so brave. Someone told him in German that we were all Polish and Russian labor workers, so in broken Polish, the soldier asked whether we saw any German soldiers in the area. Mama told him about the night before, when the German soldiers slept there. She pointed to the direction in which the German soldiers headed that morning. The American soldier then told us we were free, and should come out to the road.

When we came out of our hole, the sun was so bright it hurt my eyes. After a few seconds, I squinted through the sunlight and saw a long line of American tanks with soldiers climbing out. They threw candy from the tanks. Surrounded by fellow forced laborers and American soldiers, I watched the candy fly through the air. I listened to the cheers and allowed the jubilation to swallow me up. Then in an unlikely moment of solitude, overcome by the bliss that only freedom can tender, I simply stood there and cried.

Workers hugged each other. Some kissed the soldiers' boots in appreciation for freeing us. The soldier in charge gathered us together and formally informed us that we were "liberated," and the Germans couldn't force us to work for nothing any longer. The soldiers told Mama that General Patton's army liberated us. Following the Battle of the Bulge, "in one of the great moves of the war, Patton turned what was his Third Army's axis of advance through ninety degrees and set it upon the south of the German forces. The German salient was reduced by the end of January 1945, and the remainder of the process of closing up to the Rhine could be completed."[7]

At that point, the Allies had the upper hand and momentum was on their side. By March 7, 1945, the Allies had taken Cologne and established a bridge across the Rhine at Remagen. They pushed eastward toward us surrounding the Germans in the Ruhr on April 1 and moved farther into Germany where they liberated the infamous Buchenwald concentration camp on April 12.[8] Although the Nazis technically classified Buchenwald as a forced labor camp like ours, many of the prisoners were exterminated or died from the harsh treatment they received there, all for no other reason than that they were Jews.

Following our liberation, the American soldiers went looking for the German labor-camp bosses. They were found hiding, as we were. The soldiers ordered them to come out. Reluctantly, they complied, but they didn't appear as grateful or happy to be discovered as we were. A German boy came up to me and, in an attempt to show me some kindness, offered me his belt with a swastika on it. I said, "No, thanks. What would I need that for?"

The excitement around us was building. I rejoiced with the indescribable joy of freedom. The soldiers announced that all of the liberated laborers would be given twenty-four hours of pure freedom, an opportunity to do whatever they wanted without risk of punishment, proclaimed the soldier in charge. The results of that announcement played out in a strange form of organized chaos. Each person used his or her freedom in different ways. Some immediately took the opportunity to kill German civilians who had horribly mistreated them for so long. Others robbed wine cellars; breaking bottles and drinking excessively. Polish women who had collaborated with the Germans got their heads shaved. Former slave laborers then forced them to march through town in a humiliating exercise, where onlookers threw rocks and sticks, laughed, and spit on them.

The twenty-four-hour period passed, and with the pent-up vengeance mostly purged, the soldiers laid out the options available to the liberated slave laborers. American soldiers told us that they could not provide transportation for us, because they needed all their equipment to continue fighting the war, so they instructed us to go to the nearest Displaced People's (DP) camp in Saalfeld Saale. Mama and Andrzej took turns holding Leon and walked an entire day without food or water. I followed along, despite not completely having regained all of my strength from my kidney infection.

As we walked, we came across downed bridges. Roads were littered with dead German soldiers and civilians, their lifeless corpses void of any feeling except the expression frozen on their faces, an expression that conveyed the terror of their final few moments. Their mouths gaped open. Their eyes, some were closed. Some cried out with a silent stare into nowhere. Some of the bodies lay untouched on the ground. Others we passed were mutilated or dismembered. They rested in awkward positions on the blood-stained earth. We stepped past one of them, and my foot landed in a puddle of blood that was still somewhat fresh. I kept walking, to keep pace with my mother, but I looked behind me at a trail of bloody footprints my shoes left for three or four steps. The bodies and the blood made me a bit uneasy, but my senses grew numb to the sight within a few minutes. We had already been through so much that almost nothing alarmed us by then.

We made our way through the forest across rivers and streams, including a winding river at two locations in our journey. At the first impasse, we stood at the river's edge, about six feet above the water line, and watched the current rush toward the bank. We stared at the white caps that moved swiftly past us. The current crashed water into the bank before us, and the waves curled back, dragging anything it pulled along deep down below the surface. One of the men, determined not to let "a little water hold us up," got down on his hands and knees. With the help of two of the others, he climbed over the bank and steadied his footing on a rock, while maintaining a firm grip on one of the tree roots protruding from the side of the riverbank. Eventually we got better at navigating across these impediments. When we reached the second crossing, the adults made a human chain, clasping hands through the river. Andrzej carried my brother and me on his shoulders at one point. When we approached the other side, we crawled over the shoulders of the adults, one to another. Sometimes the adults released their grip from the human chain, raising their hands over their heads to guide the smallest of the children until we were safely placed on the other side. Exhausted and hungry, we arrived at the camp in the evening.

In Saalfeld Saale, hundreds of displaced people from Poland, Russia, and other countries gathered in a school. American soldiers were nowhere to be seen. They were still fighting the war. Wall-to-wall drunk people greeted us to join the celebration of our collective freedom. I could hear the wine bottles breaking all around me. Even with all the noise and excitement, I couldn't help thinking about the American soldier who liberated us. His clean-shaven face. His waxed mustache. How could he have been so clean, and yet fight in this dirty war?

The evening was joyfully chaotic. At eleven years old, I got drunk for the first time in my life, sipping the remainders in almost-empty wine bottles. When Mama discovered me, she sent me to bed, and my celebration abruptly ended. I rambled in gibberish and headed off to our room. We slept in a school that night, on a pile of straw laid out on the floor. Lying on my straw bed, I watched the ceiling as it spun around and around.

The next day, the soldiers provided us a room at a German military camp. We had showers, beds, and a pristine place to sleep. With such an extraordinary improvement in our living conditions, I wondered how long it would last.

CHAPTER 11
FROM ONE PLACE TO ANOTHER

After a few days, I saw the significant presence of American soldiers. To see these men in increasing number and frequency helped the reality of my freedom sink in. I can't properly put into words how it felt to become free. An intense stress that pressed down on me every single day had been lifted. I felt the physical relief in my eyes as I looked at my surroundings in a more relaxed way. The pressure in my head and the adrenaline that frequently shocked my heart no longer infected my body. *"I'm free!"* I yelled as loudly as I could in my mind. I stopped, at one point, in no particular place and took a deep breath. I inhaled slowly and took in every scent that passed my nose, not wanting to take anything for granted. Running around Saalfeld Saale circle for the first time in my life, I listened to a live concert offered by American soldiers. It consumed me. I was overwhelmed, gaping in awe, sitting on the ground and listening to a live orchestra. *"I'm free!"* I was mesmerized, and for a moment, forgot the ugly remnants of the war. I snapped out of my daze and realized it was getting dark, so I rushed back to the camp. I didn't want to have to confront any ghosts. On the way, I saw an old German woman pushing a wagon full of hay up the hill. She reminded me of my grandmother in Poland, so I stopped and asked her if she needed help.

"Oh, yes," she said in German.

As she pulled the wagon and I pushed from the back, she asked me where I lived. I told her that I was Polish and lived in the DP camp. When we got to the top of the hill, she thanked me and said she could manage.

I ran back to the camp. Mama was happy to see me, for she thought I got lost. A few weeks later, that old woman came to the camp looking for me. I wasn't there to greet her. I was out playing with two fourteen-year-old girls I befriended when we moved to Saalfeld Saale. When I got home, Mama showed me two dainty, hand-embroidered handkerchiefs, one in pink and another in blue. She said that the German woman made them as repayment for my good deed. I felt surprised that a German woman would do such a thing, because until then, such an act was almost unheard of.

With nothing to do one day, several kids, including Leon and I, invaded a neighboring fruit garden. We made a hole in the fence and ate our fill of several kinds of fruit before the German farmer came running down the hill with a pitchfork, screaming at us in German. Some kids who made their way to the tops of the fruit trees were caught. Most of us stayed on the ground, and we escaped. Some who could not find the opening in the fence were also caught, Leon included. The farmer did not hurt them, but scolded them while we waited helplessly, peeking through the hole in the fence from the side of the road.

The soldiers soon recognized that the lack of food presented an escalating problem. With no means of providing enough food for the masses, they threw grenades into the Saale River, causing a multitude of fish to float to the surface. Mama ran to the river to pick some of the fish, but did not realize how deep the river was. She lost her footing and the strong current carried her downstream. She almost drowned. In her scramble to get to shore and pull herself up the riverbank, she lost the cross of Jesus that she had carried in her bra throughout the war. Mama eventually got her fish, a pail full, which she lugged over to me.

"Start cleaning them," she instructed.

I never saw fish before, and I was reluctant to handle them. I poked at one for a minute or so, with my upper lip curled, trying to get used to the concept of actually picking one up. Eventually I opened my hand and reached for one. They were so slimy that I could not get a firm grip. Finally someone else came and took over, gutting and cutting the heads off the slippery, bug-eyed creatures. I watched the process from a distance, still not particularly warm to the idea of this "fish thing."

The soldiers, with the help of the freed laborers, cooked the fish on a fireplace they built from stray stones that lay on the ground. On top of the fire they laid a makeshift grill from a spool of wire. When the fish was cooked, Mama presented my portion to me. I looked around to see if anyone else was going to eat it. The way the adults devoured it, I supposed that it couldn't be too bad.

My first taste was an experience in itself. With some degree of caution, I picked up a large piece of the fish with both hands and bit in, swallowing hard. My eyes watered and my cheeks turned red as I coughed and gasped for air. After gagging for what seemed like an eternity, I regained my composure to learn that fish have bones. I was reminded of this lesson every day, while the bone stayed lodged in my throat for months, literally.

The grounds at the Saalfeld Saale camp overflowed with refugees, and the Polish people were afraid to return to what was by then Communist Poland. We, as liberated forced laborers, had a great deal to celebrate, but Poland as a country did not. At the Yalta conference in February 1945, as the war's end drew near, U.S. President Franklin D. Roosevelt, UK Prime Minister Winston Churchill, and USSR Premier Joseph Stalin met to discuss the post-war reorganization of Europe, particularly of the countries conquered by Germany. Stalin considered Poland to be a key country of interest. In the negotiations, he argued:

"...throughout history, Poland has been the corridor through which the enemy has passed into Russia. Twice in the last thirty years, our enemies, the Germans, have passed through this corridor. It is in Russia's interest that Poland should be strong and powerful, in a position to shut the door of this corridor by her own force.... It is necessary that Poland should be free, independent in power. Therefore, it is not only a question of honor but of life and death for the Soviet state."

Stalin's stance on Poland was non-negotiable. By the end of the seven-day conference, Roosevelt and Churchill reluctantly agreed to Stalin's proposal with a stipulation tendered by Churchill that allowed for free elections in Poland, a promise that Stalin consented to, but would not keep. Under Communist law, Poland simply moved from one bad situation to another.

When the war formally ended, we saw many wounded German soldiers walking the streets in and around Saalfeld Saale, with their hand extended for help of any kind. Ironically, they were so poor that they were willing to beg from the same people they had mistreated so terribly. We had nothing to give. Many of those soldiers were missing one or both arms or even a leg. It was a horrible sight. I watched them from a distance and wondered, *"Were these the same soldiers we so feared all this time?"*

Mama was eager to go back to America, as were other American citizens. In an effort to expedite our passage to the United States, she spent most of her time speaking to the authorities at the various camps that sprung up. Unfortunately, the DPs descended upon these camps faster and in greater number than the military was prepared to handle. The camp organizers, therefore, could not provide a comprehensive process to expedite our quick departure. When Mama wasn't speaking to camp authorities, she listened to the conversations of fellow DPs in hopes that she could gather more information on how to get us across the ocean. We shuffled from one place to another, crossing paths with other DPs, day after day, as the camp administrators struggled to maintain order.

A few weeks passed, and Mama read a notice on the board outside our sleeping area. American soldiers had been instructed to relinquish the area to the Soviet Union, including the Saalfeld Saale camp. We had a choice: to stay and live under Communist rule or leave with the Americans. It was not a difficult decision. We chose to go. We weren't alone. Almost nobody wanted to stay behind if the U.S. military was leaving. We all followed the U.S. soldiers to other DP camps they managed. Having heard the stories of how Stalin's troops were treating civilians, most people were merely trying to get out of Germany before the Russians arrived. Thankfully, American soldiers quickly mobilized trucks and within days shipped us all to Coburg, a town about an hour southwest of Saalfeld Saale.

The night before the trucks arrived, soldiers told us to be up and ready to go before sunrise. For each truck that pulled up at our barracks, one soldier instructed us to quickly pile in, as many as we could fit. We jumped in, once again, like sardines, with a canopy roof over our heads. It was a tight squeeze, and it reminded me of being in the cattle cars on the way to the slave labor camp. The only difference was that the anxiety and panic that accompanied us on the trip to the labor camp was replaced with excitement for what was in store for us, as we got closer and closer to America.

After getting settled in our temporary home, I roamed around the area to get myself acquainted with my new surroundings. I watched the American soldiers, only from a distance, though. Although so appreciative of what they had done for us, I was respectful of their mission and particularly of the artillery they carried. Two groups of soldiers stood casually on a smoke break. White soldiers made up one of the groups. Another group contained only black soldiers. I thought it odd that although the two groups wore the same uniform, they did not interact. I watched for a while, but then never gave it a second thought.

Mama inquired about sending me to school, but they were too far from our camp. After a few weeks in Coburg, I contracted chicken pox and was quarantined. Mama walked me with my red, pimpled face to the infirmary, and the nurse showed me to a small room with a single window, in a barracks with a bunk bed and brown blanket. The walls were cold, made of old wooden planks. The nurse led me in. Mama and I looked at each other. I couldn't hug her, because she was afraid to contract the virus and give it to little Leon. The nurse closed the door and left me there all alone. I walked over to the bed, pulled the blanket over myself, and cried. For ten days, they held me in the infirmary. Mama was not allowed to visit me in my room. Hospital staff delivered food to me on a tray through a small opening. The sense of loneliness tortured me every moment I was awake. I was a prisoner again, but this time, I was all alone.

During those days, I slept much of the time. When I was awake I often lay in my bed, looking up at the ceiling and crying. Other times, I sat by the window, imagining myself on the other side of the glass. I watched people milling around, not doing anything in particular. They stood around, waiting for something, anything. Every few days, Mama appeared at my window to wave and smile. She got as close as she could, despite the bushes that kept her at arm's length. When I saw her, I rushed to the window and smiled back. We'd stare at each other, maybe mouth a few words, but that was all. Her visits were never long, but they always lifted my spirits.

While in Coburg, Mama saw the Polish foreman, Tomasz and his family in the same camp. It sent chills up her spine to recall how he had treated his fellow Poles at Heinrich's farm, how he sided with the Nazis, and how he beat her so ruthlessly. Enraged, Mama went to the MPs and told them her story.

"What is he doing here?" she demanded to know.

With pen and paper, they took the details from my mother like a policeman after a traffic accident. They told her they would process the paperwork and arrest him the next day.

Before his impending arrest, Mama came in contact with a priest. Among other things, she asked his advice about how to handle the situation concerning Tomasz's arrest. The priest asked her to recite the Lord's Prayer.

She paused for a moment. Then, with a puzzled expression, she began to pray. "Our Father, who art in Heaven, hallowed be Thy name."

She continued through "and forgive us our trespasses as we forgive those who trespass against us."

The priest abruptly stopped her and said, "Did you hear what you just said?"

Mama thought for a while and said, "I forgive him."

Mama went back to the MPs and told them to forget everything. Completely confused, they threw up their hands and shook their heads. Mama thanked them and walked away. As the famous saying goes, "To err is human; to forgive is divine."

The camp in Coburg was overcrowded. After a few weeks, we left there and went to Luchow, about five hours north of Coburg. Aunt Julia joined us there. Because she was healthy enough to maintain the pace of the harsh working conditions, she stayed at Heinrich's farm until the end of the war. Being a quiet and deliberate sort, Aunt Julia never really said much about her experiences after we parted. We were all just happy to be together again.

We lived in one room with another Polish girl, Anna. She was about sixteen years old and taken from her parents to work in the camps. I can scarcely imagine what she went through. Andrzej, meanwhile, no longer lived with us. His health was deteriorating, and he developed a problem breathing.

In late 1945, we transferred to another camp in Bamberg. Although Andrzej was no longer traveling with us, he made his way there somehow. When we disembarked from the train at the Bamberg station, my mouth fell open, and Mama shook her head in disbelief at the sight before us. Out in the field, ten or twenty feet from the railroad tracks, we saw German townspeople digging inside what appeared to be a vast sink hole. The hole was at least ten feet deep and spanned more than a thousand square feet. At the edge of the hole on the right side lay more than a hundred wooden caskets. From the edge of the hole, and alongside the workers down inside, American soldiers directed the activity.

With pick axes, shovels, and sometimes their bare hands, the townspeople pulled bodies from the hole and laid them into the wooden boxes. Stray arms, legs, and heads were also placed in caskets with what was best believed to be the associated body. Mama turned to the man nearest her. "What is going on here?" she demanded.

"It's a mass grave of POWs and other prisoners," the man responded. "The Nazis, including some of these townspeople, didn't want to be associated with the torture and murder that took place here, so they tried to hide what they had done. They killed the witnesses—the prisoners—and buried the evidence. Many of these bodies are American POWs. The American soldiers are forcing the local townspeople to dig the bodies out for identification and a proper burial."

We stepped away from the train platform and walked along a path that brought us closer to the hole than I cared to be. I peered inside the grave and saw the workers up close. The American soldiers spoke in German. "Dig carefully," they told the workers. "We don't want to damage the bodies any more than they already are." Three or four of the workers dug by hand. When a worker with a shovel identified a body, the hand diggers were called over to assist in the delicate process of exhuming what was, with great hope, a whole body. Most times, the discovery of a single body led to the discovery of more.

The smell overwhelmed us. I covered my nose and mouth with the sleeve of my blouse. Mama did the same with her handkerchief. Others simply threw up. We moved past the hole, maintaining pace with the other arriving DPs. At the same time, we looked back at the hole to confirm that our eyes had not deceived us. Except for when a body was brought to the surface, I saw little more than the heads of the workers while they labored at the gravesite.

The walk to our new camp in Bamberg was short. After dropping our small bag of belongings in our room, Mama went immediately to the American military bases in the area: New Marks, Hochenfeltz, and Pocking (the second largest DP camp in Germany) to search for her brother, Stanley, and sister Genevieve. Sometimes she hitched a ride on a military truck. Other times, she traveled by train. How she paid for these trips, I don't know. We didn't have any money, but Mama was never deterred by a lack of funds. She was a resourceful sort who talked her way into whatever she needed.

Aunt Julia took care of my brother Leon and me in her absence. After a few days, Mama returned to Bamberg with news that her brother and sister had already left for Poland. Along with her, Mama brought a man named Leon, whom she met in Pocking. Leon was kind and appeared quite happy. He always had a chocolate to give me, and I liked him. He was a good-looking man, but it was clear that he had seen hard times during the war. His cheek bones showed prominently and his face was drawn. His hair was prematurely grey.

He was an educated man from a well-to-do, politically connected family, so his memories of pre-war Poland were much different from mine. As a boy growing up in an affluent family outside of Warsaw, he never lacked food, clothing, or shelter like we did, yet when I think of the stories he told of his struggle to survive, I sit in awe of his ability to persevere.

I suppose that in some ways, I probably had it easier adjusting to the war than he did. When we were forced to leave Poland, our living conditions were quite deprived. Our step into forced labor, although deplorable, was not so far a departure from our pre-war days as it was for Leon. He spent most of his early adult years either fighting or running for his life from the Russians. His family had a great deal to lose, and they lost it all: their land, horses and cows, a stately home with everything in it, and high stature in the community. They left with nothing more than the clothes on their backs.

As a teenager, he followed the path of a military cadet. He joined the service as an officer. When the fighting in his hometown broke out, his family literally scattered. At twenty-four, he went to his assigned military post in Warsaw where his unit was ordered to march east. When his unit encountered westbound Russian soldiers, they exchanged fire and Leon suffered shrapnel wounds that tore his leg apart and left him lying on the battlefield. The Russians, who never signed the Geneva Convention, were under no obligation to follow it. Therefore, they did not give preferential treatment to officers. They simply shot them. Knowing this, Leon disposed of his uniform minutes before his capture. Following his arrest, Russian doctors put his leg back together with carpenter nails. Soon thereafter, Leon found himself on a prison train to Siberia.

After about a year, he escaped and walked thousands of miles, through bitter cold and treacherous terrain, into British-controlled

India. Along with other Polish pilots who escaped their homeland by the skin of their teeth, he was assigned to a British fighting unit and flew missions for the Allies until the end of the war.

We listened in awe to his story about a second escape at the end of the war, from Russian forces who were instructed to dispose of any Polish soldiers they encountered. While hiding in Hungary, afraid to return to Poland, he came face to face with Russian military men who discovered him by chance. He ran for his life into the nearby woods. Scrambling as fast as his feet could carry him, he stumbled through the dense trees, falling over the roots and loose branches that lay on the forest floor. In the distance he heard the sounds of soldiers assembling, and the thunderous rumble of boots.

He sprinted deeper and deeper into the woods, and he heard an officer shouting orders and military dogs in pursuit. The sound of restless barking got nearer, and his breathing got shorter and uneven. Panic set in. His breaths turned to faint cries of distress. They were closing in on him. Not willing to give up, he kept moving and came across a stream and then a few small brooks. He meandered through the shallow water, hoping to throw the dogs off his trail.

He told us the incredible story of how he submerged himself in the frigid waters of a raging river, breathing through a reed, while troops ran past him in pursuit. He spoke of being so cold and soaked to the skin after emerging from the river that he hallucinated while he staggered along the riverbanks. He imagined people calling to him from the deepest parts of the water, waving him in their direction, toward certain death by drowning. On one occasion, entranced by the visions, he walked waist deep into the river before breaking the spell and crawling back up the riverbank. He pressed forward, and heard the sounds of his pursuers farther and farther in the distance. The dogs eventually lost his scent, and the search was halted. We sat and listened to his entire story at that first meeting. It was hard for him to get through it. At times, while recalling the events, his hands and body shook. At other times, he broke down and cried. Our eyes watered as we watched him relive his tragedy.

When Leon finished his story, we collected ourselves, and went to visit Andrzej in the hospital. Andrzej did not look as though he was coming out of the hospital anytime soon. Mama told him that we were going to another camp and that when he got well, he should return to his wife in Poland. "She and your two daughters have probably been released from the Siberian labor camp by now," Mama supposed.

In Bamberg, we enjoyed our first Christmas celebration since leaving Poland. I decorated my first Christmas tree with shiny, metallic chocolate wrappers, which I diligently saved for just such an occasion. The simple things we collect when we have nothing! Aunt Julia borrowed a big saw and found enough wood to prepare for the winter. She and I sawed the wood into small pieces, so it could fit into the portable stove left behind from the previous residents. The stove's exhaust pipe passed through the window, and whenever we threw a match into the stove, we stood careful watch so as not to burn the barracks down. Mama continued her search for the fastest way to get to America. It seemed as though every time she arrived at a camp, administrators told her she'd have to go to another. Bamberg was no different. We stayed there for barely a few weeks.

In 1946, we traveled to Wildflecken. Our new friend, Leon, joined us on the train. He got off at one of the stops to go to the restroom, and the train took off without him. Mama didn't seem too concerned. At that time, although he was a nice man, he was merely another acquaintance. All the same, he knew where we were headed, and a few days later we were reunited.

All these camps had been former German soldier quarters. They were equipped with everything we needed: showers, portable stoves, and plenty of running water. We enjoyed some semblance of a normal life during those times. I went to a Polish school every day. I made my First Holy Communion in Wildflecken and was confirmed in the Catholic faith there. Aunt Julia and Leon lived with us in the same room. It was around that time that I acknowledged Leon as the male presence in our lives.

Leon worked in the office at the United Nations Relief and Rehabilitation Administration (UNRRA), assisting refugees and processing their paperwork. Mama stayed at home to care for little Leon. During that period, we noticed that she frequently felt ill and spent a great deal of time in bed. Only later did we realize that she was pregnant with her third child, Grace.

I was eager to begin learning, but I was nervous in the new school setting. Class was held in a large auditorium with hundreds of children from other DP families. All the children, regardless of age, sat in the same auditorium and learned general concepts, mostly arithmetic, history, science, geography, and music. Overwhelmed by the volume of children, I never became friendly with any of them. In fact, I don't recall interacting with any of them, with one exception. On the second or third day of school, I caught the eye of a familiar group of children. They were Tomasz's children, the Polish foreman on Heinrich's farm. We saw each other from across the room and stared for a few moments. We said nothing. They stared blankly at me. They must have seen the fury on my face. I wondered *"What are they doing here?"* as I recalled the beating my mother endured at the hands of their father. Recalling the story my mother told me about the military police and the priest after she encountered Tomasz, I turned away and tried to put them out of my mind.

Even during those early days of their relationship, Leon and Mama had frequent disagreements. Sometimes they were over simple things, like the day little Leon and I watched Mama's pots and pans go flying out the window. Apparently Leon didn't think they were clean enough. Sometimes their disagreements were over not-so-simple things. Leon had a roving eye. I heard accusations of infidelity frequently, such as when Mama went to visit him at the UNRRA. She entered the room to find him sitting with a female coworker in his lap. Mama returned to our room in tears and went back to bed.

Those events didn't keep little Leon and me from exploring our new environment. With a new and exciting place outside our door, little Leon and I were often out and about. It was late summer. The sun was usually shining, the clouds almost always floated high in the sky. Nothing stood in our way, and we roamed everywhere. On one of our journeys together, we found our way to the public bathhouse. The UNRRA encouraged us to wash regularly, and they converted the German Army barracks into public baths. Being filthy throughout the war, my brother and I took advantage of the opportunity to get clean and have fun at the same time.

We entered the house, a wide open room where the steam rose from the bathtubs and showers that were all along the walls. We slowly walked into the large room, surveying our surroundings. Our cheeks turned a rosy red when we moved from the dry summer air into the high humid warmth of the bathhouse. We looked around and saw a line of shiny, new steel tubs on the left side of the large room. Clean and modern showers stood on the right. Nothing but the best for what was meant for the Nazi soldiers.

We watched the few people using the facilities. Timidly and curiously, we walked around the room studying the environment. Our curiosity brought us toward the tubs, which looked like the most fun. They could easily hold an adult. For small children like Leon and me, they were like our personal swimming pools.

For a minute we stood in front of one of the tubs, just looking at it. The stainless steel handles. The faucet. The long pipe that carried the water into the basin. I imagined myself in my own bathroom. I reached forward and turned on the hot and cold water. The water came rushing out of the faucet, and a feeling of exhilaration swept through my body as though I were doing something a little devious. Once the tub was full, it didn't take much convincing to encourage Leon to play along. Clothes and all, we jumped into the tub together. Splashing each other and ducking under the water, making bubbles with the soap that was provided for us, we had great fun.

Once we had enough, we dragged ourselves out of the tub like wet dogs and, in our soaking wet clothes, sloshed over to the towels that were there for the taking. Still dripping, we wrapped the towels around our bodies and headed back to our room. All of these amenities, the baths, the tubs, showers, soap, and towels were only some of the services provided by the UNRRA. The UNRRA provided billions of U.S. dollars of rehabilitation aid. It ceased operations in the DP camps of Europe in 1947. Before closing its doors, the organization helped about eight million refugees, including our family. It provided a regular supply of clothing for our whole family, and for the first time in my life, I had a change of clothes.

One afternoon Leon and Mama came home to announce that they had gotten married. In a civil ceremony at one of the office buildings on the grounds, they exchanged vows. When they returned to tell us about it, they were matter-of-fact, as though it were simply the thing to do. Mama explained that little Leon and I had a new father. Soon thereafter, our names were changed to our stepfather's surname.

Things were finally beginning to improve for us in Wildflecken. We started to settle in. At least I did. With so much time spent sitting around, both Mama and Stepfather were always looking for something to do. Stepfather took accordion lessons. Mama pestered officials in the offices about how to get to America sooner. As long as they were busy, it eased some of the tension in the household, and everyone, including little Leon and me, were happier.

To get spending money, we got involved in the local black market. Mama and Stepfather saw that other families were out in the street selling things to make money. They asked other DPs about what goods could be sold, where they found goods to sell, and how much money could be made.

It was around Easter time. Mama and Stepfather took note of the common complaint of the local women around religious holy days. They frequently ran out of yeast for the bread they made for their celebrations. Not long after that the light bulb went on, and I began going door to door selling yeast. Yes, yeast.

Mama and Stepfather walked to town about two miles. There they purchased a big block of yeast at the local mercantile and brought it back to our room. In the room, they unwrapped the package and cut it into smaller blocks. They then rewrapped those smaller blocks in paper that had the same feel as newsprint, tightly wrapped so that it wouldn't unravel.

The black market was illegal. If adults were caught, they were punished and the goods were confiscated. Getting caught certainly would hinder Mama and Stepfather's plans of getting to America. On the other hand, to catch a child selling black market goods was seen as a lesser offense, especially a blond-haired little girl.

They placed five or six blocks of yeast into a small bag and sent me on my way. I carried only about five or six pieces at a time, which allowed me to conceal it if necessary. It was also all they could afford to buy at one time. I walked to each building, one by one. They all looked about the same, so I got into a routine fairly quickly. I walked up the stairs to the front entrance of the building, opened the heavy double door, and walked inside. I walked up the stairs to the first landing and yelled, "Yeast for sale! Yeast for sale!"

My voice echoed in the empty hallway. The first time I did it, I was apprehensive. I yelled, and nobody came. I waited for a few minutes and listened. Nothing. I yelled again. "Yeast for sale! Yeast for sale!" A door opened, to my surprise, and a woman appeared. She handed me a crumpled bill, a German mark. I handed her the small package, careful not to unravel it as it went from my hand to hers. With money in hand, I happily scampered up to the next floor.

After a few sales, my apprehension dissipated and I took a liking to my new job. The routine was always the same. In the big door, up the stairs, then up the next flight, all the while, yelling, "Yeast for sale! Yeast for sale!" Of all of the people I came across, I don't remember any of the faces. This was illegal business. It was conducted quickly, with little said and few, if any, pleasantries exchanged. To be perfectly honest, I loved doing it.

When the baking season was over and demand for yeast dwindled, Mama and Stepfather went to factories and brought handbags back to the room. I sold those, too. After a while, we stopped participating in the black market, having been reminded how a fourteen-year-old Polish boy selling cigarettes was shot by American soldiers. When they ordered him to stop, he ran instead. We went to the viewing, and everyone cried hysterically.

By that point, our lives showed noticeable signs of improvement. The UNRRA fed and clothed us well enough, certainly better than we were used to. I saw people everywhere I turned, day and night. While walking around one winter day, I came across a man who was about forty years old. The snow was piled high around the camp, and he was jumping back and forth over the snow banks. As he jumped in and out of view, I could hear him screaming profanities about the war. It concerned me enough that I stayed closer to "home" for the rest of the time we lived there.

By that time, complaining and impatient, Mama went to the Immigration office. The officer at the counter told Mama that her husband Leon's papers were not in order. "Furthermore," he said, "because he is not an American citizen, it will take even longer for him to get approval to travel." The officer advised her to move to yet another camp for only Americans, where the competition to travel was lighter.

We moved to Niederrad Frankfurt Am Main, a more private camp. The provisions were more plentiful, and facilities more upscale than we were used to. Stepfather joined the Polish Military Services, and we did not see him often. In a way, I was happy to be free from the now-common beatings, scolding, and arguments over matters I perceived as insignificant. We were provided a small, well-furnished, clean apartment. German soldiers must have lived there, for the basement was filled with German propaganda and literature.

I went to an American school with other children during the day. I wanted to learn English quickly, so in the evening, I also attended English classes with the adults. I had an old German teacher who was also going back to America. Her class was always full. Learning the language came easy for me. Having a strong foundation in the German language helped me excel.

On June 9, 1947, Mama gave birth to Grace, and I was thrilled to have a little sister in my life. A perfect baby, Grace hardly cried. Mama nursed her, but produced more milk than Grace required, so the hospital gave Mama a pump to extract the milk for their German premature babies. Mama agreed to pump, but we found it to be a little unsettling, knowing that the parents of some of these children were outright Nazi supporters. It bothered me even more that I was sent by trolley to carry the milk to the hospital for these children, every day.

Days and weeks went by. Mama grew increasingly frustrated with all of the waiting around to get to America. Our papers were not being processed fast enough, and she frequently visited the immigration office to complain. Each time, they politely asked for her patience and sent her away.

CHAPTER 12
PATIENCE, PRAYER
AND PERSISTENCE

In late 1947, we moved to Butzbach. Grace was but a few months old. Mama learned that negotiating through this camp might get us on a boat to America. Aunt Julia joined us there. In Butzbach, an outbreak of influenza erupted, and Grace got sick. The morning that she awoke with a fever, Mama and Stepfather grew concerned because the virus was spreading quickly throughout the camp. They told me to stay with Leon while they brought Grace to the infirmary, a barracks that was set up with a few beds as a temporary location to care for the sick. The doctors diagnosed her immediately and sent her to the hospital, where she spent several weeks.

Doctors gave instructions to place her in quarantine. We all walked to the hospital to visit Grace often, although from a distance. To see her, we walked into the main hospital entrance where Mama or Stepfather requested that Grace be brought to the window. When the nurse brought her to the window, she usually just lay there, asleep. We mostly talked to each other, always facing toward the baby as we spoke. I looked through the window at her and wished I could hold my baby sister, but children were strictly forbidden to be directly exposed to the virus.

After her first week in the hospital, with no improvement in her condition, Mama decided to baptize her there, in the hospital. I was chosen to be the godmother, and Stepfather's brother, Wladyslaw in France, was added to the certificate as the godfather. It was an odd ceremony, where the resident nurse held Grace, while the on-site priest administered the baptismal rite with traditional oils, prayers, and water. All the while, Mama, Stepfather, Leon, and I watched from the other side of the glass. The ceremony took about ten minutes. In Grace's weakened condition, she barely moved, except to twitch when the priest poured the cold baptismal water over her forehead.

We headed home after the baptism and constantly prayed, as a family in our room, at the church on the grounds, and privately each morning and night. Over the subsequent weeks, we worried as we heard about an increasing number of young children dying from the illness. Finally, with the round-the-clock care and medicine, Grace's condition slowly improved. In time, she regained some of her strength, her fever broke, and the hospital released her. It was a big relief for all of us.

In Butzbach, Mama searched unsuccessfully for a Polish or English school where she could enroll me. For a while, I took private English lessons from a German woman. Stepfather negotiated to pay her with the UNRRA coffee rations we received that were piling up in our room. Even though we hadn't gotten accustomed to drinking coffee, we never threw anything away. With so little in our possession, we were always working to conserve resources. Whatever we were given, if we didn't consume it, we kept it, on the chance that it had some value in trade.

For each half-hour lesson, my English instructor recited vocabulary words and sentences to me, and I repeated them back to her. Recalling my lessons back in Niederrad, I always thought that she pronounced the words incorrectly, but went along with the lessons because, as a child, I was not in a position to correct my instructor. "Cecylia, repeat after me, 'Mun-dee, Toos-dee, Vensdee..."' I reluctantly repeated the words, with a sour look on my face, somehow knowing that an American would never speak like that.

In the fall of that year, Mama and Stepfather decided to put me in a regular German school. While apprehensive, as the only Polish student there, I liked that school. Everyone was friendly. I hoped and prayed that, finally I could be around German children without them picking on me or making fun of me.

As a Roman Catholic, I of course was enrolled in the Catholic religion classes taught by the priests. After a few weeks, and as my new friendships blossomed, some of the other kids asked me to come with them to their Protestant catechism classes, something of which few Catholics, at that time, would approve. To please both my mother and my new friends, I decided to attend the Catholic classes one day and the Protestant classes the next. The Protestant classes offered a nice change from my usual routine. They seemed to sing much more than the Catholics did. After I attended for a few days, the minister in the Protestant class approached me and asked me questions in a curious, inquisitive way. He was kind to me, but my shyness caused me to instantly freeze in his presence.

"What is your name?"

"Oh, no! The last thing I want is for my parents to find out that I've been attending Protestant catechism classes."

"Cecylia," my voice trembled.

"Where do you live?"

"Oh, my goodness! He's going to talk with my mother," I worried.

"In the Displaced People's camp, sir."

"How old are you?"

"I'm thirteen."

Although I'm sure he had many more questions, he could see that I was squirming with fright, so he backed off. As much as I wanted to tag along with my friends, the thought of having to explain my reason for forgoing my catechism classes to attend those of another religion was enough to keep me out of that class for good.

Our general studies were taught by Professor Wolf. He often read to us. Sometimes he substituted my name in the story, and we all had a good laugh. I don't remember his doing that with any of the other kids. Perhaps he liked to watch my face turn shades of red. The first time he did it, I was astounded and amused. Things were finally going so well. I was really starting to feel welcome; like one of the gang. The feeling was new and wonderful.

One morning after a freshly fallen snow, I stood at the schoolhouse steps watching the excitement as some of the children played. The snow was rich, wet, and heavy, perfect for making snowmen, sliding around, and throwing snowballs.

I casually turned to my left and, from out of nowhere, a snowball hit me squarely in the eye. I put my hands up over my face to feel whether my eye was still in its socket. The pain seared through my body, while the snow dripped down my hair and cheeks.

More than the physical pain, I was disappointed at the thought that the friendship and delicate trust that was finally being built with the German children was, in my mind, destroyed. I was angry at myself for being duped once more, and hurt that nobody came to my aid. I withdrew from the school yard fun and games, and my relationship with the other kids quickly cooled. My eye was bloodshot for weeks, and each day I went to school with that embarrassing reminder of what had happened. As I grew older, I reasoned that it was probably a random act, and I should not have taken it personally. Still, it was years before I could honestly let my guard down to another German person.

In Niederrad, Frankfurt, as well as in Butzbach, I attended Christmas parties for kids. They usually took place at hospitals with many wounded American soldiers lying in beds or sitting in wheelchairs. Others walked slowly through the hallways. Most of them were bandaged on one part of their body or another. Some were missing an arm or leg.

The parties were organized in the same general format. The party planners gathered us into a large hall modestly decorated for the season with wreaths and bows in green and red, silver and gold. Many of the soldiers who were well enough to leave their beds sat with us. At one party in Niederrad, people filled the room and the crowd swelled to well over a hundred. The atmosphere was festive with everyone conversing, laughing, and telling stories. Over the noise of the crowd, one of the organizers announced a Christmas play that was about to begin. Although the mood was bright, the sights of so many seriously wounded soldiers made it difficult for me to get into the spirit of the season. It was heart wrenching.

From the stage, the organizers handed out gifts that were said to be given by the soldiers. Most of the children rushed to the stage, but I stayed back. With the condition of the soldiers, I felt as though I should be giving gifts to them, rather than the other way around. I eventually approached the stage and received a pencil and notebook. I was happy to receive them, but my happiness was tempered by my concern for the soldiers.

Once the gifts were handed out, the organizers announced that we should be seated so the play could begin. The actors in the play were all local kids from the displaced families in the camp. A few weeks before Christmas, some of the organizers visited each of the barracks to invite any and all children to take part. One of them came to our room to invite me, but I was too shy to get up on stage, so I declined.

The play opened, and as instructed, the children walked into the hall. Each child, dressed in a white angel costume, carried a lit candle. They entered the room in single file, singing a traditional Christmas song in English. I watched them walk by me, and I noticed that one particular ten-year-old girl was holding her candle unusually close to her face. I was surprised that it didn't singe her hair.

In a split second, the flame from the candle shot up along her strands of hair and engulfed her head in fire. Before anyone could react, her porcelain face was scorched. She screamed wildly. Adults ran to her and frantically patted the flames out with their hands and any nearby cloth. A collective cry of distress arose from the crowd. In unison, as the stage curtain closed and everyone realized what had happened, the audience members all got up and exited the hall in an orderly manner, to give those who were helping the girl the space they needed. I followed the others back to our barracks. What was meant to be an enjoyable event ended in tragedy.

After several months we got word that because Aunt Julia was single and American-born, she would be the first in our family allowed to leave for the States. She made arrangements for travel to Niagara Falls, where her brother Walter and Babcia's sister, Aunt Agatha, lived.

A few months after that, with bits of information collected here and there, Mama devised a plan. If she requested passage to America with her children only, permission would be granted almost immediately. Furthermore, she knew that once she reached the United States, she would be supported by the U.S. welfare system. She heard that a single mother with three children in the United States on welfare would certainly be questioned as to how she planned to support her family. To announce that her husband was awaiting approval to come to the United States so that he could support the family might be the fastest way to expedite the processing of his papers. She went back to the immigration office and adjusted her request to include passage for her and her children only. The plan worked. She packed, and soon thereafter, we left by train for Bremen, a holding area for the harbor city that was overflowing with emigrants.

We arrived in the late afternoon. We disembarked, and I found the hustle and bustle of the hundreds of people exciting. The industrial sights and sounds of an active train station were all around. As we made our way through the crowd, I kept my eyes on Mama, who carried our bag in one hand and Grace in the other. Leon was my responsibility, and I held his hand so tightly that my knuckles were white and his fingers were blue.

We made our way through the throngs of people, and I took my eyes off Mama long enough to watch the trains chugging in and out of the station and the dark billows of smoke they left behind. I saw conductors in their blue uniforms directing passengers one way or the other. One conductor called out to anyone in earshot, *"Alle an bord!"*

Over the loudspeaker I heard a voice announcing arrivals and departures to places I'd never heard of. So many people. Some all by themselves, carrying little more than a small satchel. Others had large families with three or more children in tow, not to mention the beat-up suitcases and trunks. After going through our usual course of identification and processing, we were given our temporary living quarters in another German barracks, where we bedded down for the night.

Within a few weeks, they transported us by truck to the port city of Bremerhaven.

CHAPTER 13
A NEW HOME

On the morning of April 7, 1948, we left for the United States. Mama woke me up early. Even though our dream was finally coming true, we were too exhausted from the trip, the transfers, and the lugging of bags and children to show any excitement. We gathered the few things we had with us and followed the crowd of people toward the ship that promised to take us across the Atlantic.

Before boarding, we waited in a long line to present our papers. Mama had everything prepared and in order. She resolved to get us on that boat. When we got to the front of the line, Mama confidently placed our papers on the desk in front of the ship's immigration agent and looked him right in the eyes. Although she displayed all of the confidence of a born-and-bred American, she later told me her stomach did somersaults while she anxiously waited for the agent to review the documents, one at a time. Mama answered his questions as he looked us over, one by one. After what seemed like an eternity, the agent handed her back the papers and said, "Enjoy your trip."

The line to board the ship was long. We followed the people in front of us in a slow moving queue, up the gangplank, and onto the ship. We ambled up the incline, and my eyes must have been the size of saucers as I took note of the enormity of the vessel we were boarding. I studied it from one end to the other. The name *Marine Jumper* was written on the side of the boat. I said it to myself a few times. "*Marine Jumper. Marine Jumper.*" Years before, Babcia told me that the more smokestacks on a boat, the faster it travels, so I made a point of noting how many our boat had. There were two of them.

At the top of the gangplank, the ship steward greeted us and escorted us to cabin number A16 on the second level of the ship. When he opened the door, we peeked inside, and were impressed at how clean and well prepared the cabin looked. The bed linens were crisp and carefully tucked under the mattress. It was a small cabin with two bunk beds on each side of the room.

"Dinner will be served at six this evening," the steward informed us. Before he turned to leave he added, "Let me know if you need anything else."

Mama thanked him.

He smiled, nodded, and closed the cabin door.

With a sigh of relief, Mama dropped down onto the bed with Grace by her side. For Leon and me, the excitement was only beginning, and we were gearing up for it. I took Leon over to the porthole on the outer wall between the two bunk beds. He was not yet tall enough to look out the window on his own. I lifted him and we both pressed our faces to the glass window and peered out over the water. We waited in the room, and after some time, we heard the ship's horn blow.

Finally, on a refugee-packed boat, we set out to sea. As the steward instructed, we went down to dinner at six. The menu that evening, and throughout the trip, was outstanding. I had never tasted such delicious food in my life. It truly felt like paradise and near to heaven. After a few days of swaying on the ocean, we were instructed to take part in drills in case of an emergency. We learned how to use a life preserver. We also were instructed on how to unfasten and release the lifeboats into the water. They taught us how to board them in an orderly manner. They identified group leaders who would guide and steer the boats away from a sinking ship once they were filled with people.

Leon, six, watched all the hustle and bustle. He finally asked me, "What's going on?"

As a joke, I foolishly screamed, "The ship is sinking!"

Terrified, the poor kid instantly wet his pants. Mama scolded me ruthlessly, and I deserved it.

It was lot of fun to be on the ship while it made its way to the wide-open ocean, swaying back and forth, making everyone else sick. At times Leon and I were the only ones in the dining room. Plates and glasses rolled off the tables and broke constantly. Mama, seasick and visibly pregnant with another child, could hardly get up. She and Grace stayed in bed most of the time.

For almost ten days we cruised toward our destination. When we arrived in New York Harbor in the late afternoon, the ship was not allowed to dock. The line of ships ahead of us was too long. We waited through the rest of the afternoon. The sun slowly made its way behind the distant buildings. Evening came, and we were still in the harbor, awaiting access to the port.

Standing on the deck of the boat, from the distance I saw the New York City skyline lit up with thousands of bright, colorful lights. I wondered what it was. It looked like a slice of heaven, a wonderland of all my dreams come true. The glare of the skyline lights bounced off the water, making it shine like a thousand stars. The lights and the glare blended so brightly that I could barely distinguish where the land stopped and where the water started. A state of euphoria overcame me. I thought about my future and could see only wonderful things happening to me. What a change from the past several years when we knew only struggle and hardship! It was fascinating and bewildering. My spirit soared in wonderment and curiosity, mixed with a little anxiety. At almost fourteen years old, how was I going to fit in, in a new country where I knew almost nothing about the language or the people?

Thoughts raced through my mind. Throughout the night, I dozed off long enough for the next thought to stir me up again. In the early morning, as the sun rose, I went back up on deck. I looked up over the ship's bow and saw the Statue of Liberty. I knew nothing about her. She was peeking in and out of the morning fog. At times I could see her chest. At other times, I saw her face and her arm that held the torch that glowed through the mist. At times she looked as though she hung suspended in midair. Someone who must have seen me staring at her in an almost trance-like state stood alongside me and, in a church whisper, explained the significance of the Lady and all that she meant to America, particularly to people like us.

After a long, seemingly endless day of waiting, the next evening approached and we followed the throngs of people off the ship. With so many passengers disembarking, the process took hours, with multiple passport and verification checks. Once we got off the boat, we saw the chaos of immigration officers, New York City port greeters, United Relief organizers, and cab drivers interacting with the hundreds of arriving passengers.

Mama was overwhelmed by the chaos, and her pregnant body was exhausted, so we plopped our luggage down in the middle of the landing and sat. According to our papers, we were expected to board a train, courtesy of the UNRRA, and follow the same path that Aunt Julia had taken, to Niagara Falls to live with Mama's brother Walter and Aunt Agatha. Over the course of our journey, however, Mama decided on a change in plans. We would wait in New York until Stepfather arrived. The big questions were where we would stay and how we would afford it.

We sat until Mama regained her strength, at which point she handed Grace to me and told me to watch Leon so she could go gather information. A few hours later, which to me was an eternity, she returned with papers in hand. Before I knew it, we were shoveled into the back seat of a yellow taxi and taken to the Hotel Chelsea on the west side of Manhattan.

The hotel had an elegant lobby with red carpets and ornately decorated walls with elaborate paintings. We were given a room on the seventh floor, again funded by the UNRRA. The porter took our bags and led us up to our room. It was my first trip in an elevator, a luxury I seldom employed, unless accompanied by others, for fear that I would get stuck. The seven flights of stairs were fine, as far as I was concerned.

We arrived at our room, and in the same manner as when we were shown to our cabin on the ship, Mama, with Grace in her arms, dropped her exhausted body onto one of the comfortable beds. Leon and I ran to the window. Looking out to the streets below, I was amazed at the volume of traffic, the number of yellow taxis, and the flickering lights of the RKO movie theatre: Now Playing, James Stewart in *Call Northside 777*. After a few moments, exhaustion overtook our excitement. Leon and I soon followed Mama's lead, pulling off our sweat-filled shoes, lying down on the bed and drifting off to sleep for the night.

The next morning we awoke to the sounds of the busy New York City streets. We could hear the hustle and bustle on the avenue below, the sounds of the cars, the horns, the voices of people here and there. My eyes opened, and I arose with a start. After a refreshing night's sleep, I was ready for the next step in our journey. We all were. Mama's first order of business was to find money. She knew our time at the hotel was limited, and she wanted to use that time wisely.

Each day she left early in the morning and was usually gone all day looking for some sort of financial help, while I took care of Leon and Grace. On her first day out in the New York metropolis, she returned well after dark. I was worried and wondered what had happened. She explained that she got terribly lost, but managed to get some monetary help from Catholic Charities. With some of the money she bought each of us new outfits, so we no longer looked like the paupers that we were. After a week or two, a hotel representative, instructed by the UNRRA, informed Mama that we no longer could stay in the hotel, and that we had to go to our family in Niagara Falls. We had no choice. With some of the money given by Catholic Charities, Mama purchased train tickets for each of us.

Once again we packed ourselves into the back seat of a yellow taxi and headed to the Pennsylvania train station en route to Niagara Falls. At the Niagara Falls train station, we were greeted by Aunt Agatha, who brought us to an apartment that she and Uncle Walter arranged for us.

Uncle Walter and Aunt Agatha were financially comfortable and agreed to help us get by until Mama found work. The apartment was immaculate, cabinets full of food, a basement full of coal and wood to last for at least a while. They were generous, and we were appreciative.

I had never met Aunt Agatha or her family before. I remembered Uncle Walter a little. I was almost four when he left Poland for America in 1938. That evening we went to dinner at Aunt Agatha's home. After dinner, Uncle Walter and his common-law wife came to greet us.

"Where did you get those beautiful clothes? You don't look deprived," Uncle Walter's wife commented.

Little did she know.

After a short while, Uncle Walter left and returned with Aunt Julia, Mama's sister. She had come to the States in 1947 from the camp in Butzbach and found work as a cleaning woman in Niagara Falls for a funeral director. He paid her twenty-five cents an hour plus room and board. It wasn't much, but it was certainly better than anywhere else she had been for the prior several years. What an exciting family reunion we had! Mama and Aunt Julia recounted the stories of the war and shared memories of our struggles and our journey to the States. They talked for hours, and Aunt Agatha and Uncle Walter listened in amazement.

Once we got settled into our apartment, I was enrolled in public school. It was the middle of May and an awkward time for me. Because of my poor English and because I arrived so late in the school year, I was placed in a sixth-grade class instead of the eighth grade with other children my age. I made the best of it, but I didn't enjoy myself.

Mama spent her days caring for Leon and Grace and doing her best to conserve energy for the afternoons that lay ahead. Each day, when I returned home from school, Mama left to pound the pavement in search of work. She was at quite a disadvantage. With two small children at home and nobody else to care for them until I returned home from school, her employment options were limited to the night shift. Her options were further limited because few employers wanted to hire a pregnant woman.

Within several weeks, Mama got a notice that Stepfather was in New York City at Ellis Island. He arrived on a ship named *Marine Flasher* and sent word that he was not coming to Niagara Falls. He wrote that he had a job and an apartment, and that we should come back to New York City. With all sorts of explanations, apologies, and pleas for forgiveness to her family who had done so much for us, Mama said that we had to go back to New York City. The family was terribly disappointed.

When we met up with Stepfather back in New York City, he brought us to an apartment building on 602 East 11th Street where he told us about his new job as janitor for the property. The job paid literally nothing, but it came with a free two-bedroom apartment on the first floor. In the beginning we had barely enough money to get by. Most of the time, we bought our food on credit, and paid for it monthly with the meager earnings from Mama's income cleaning houses and the money Stepfather earned moonlighting at odd jobs here and there. I was given some of the menial janitorial duties which allowed Stepfather more time to search for a better-paying job. He sometimes took me with him to translate.

My parents enrolled me in a public school on the corner of 12th Street and Avenue A. It was close to the house, which I liked, but the anxiety of being in an American school lingered. Regardless, I had little time to dwell on my own feelings. When the school day ended, I rushed home to take care of Leon and Grace and do homework, in between. In the evening, my chores around the house and the janitorial duties for which I was responsible kept me breathless. Time to play or time with friends did not fit into the schedule. Thank goodness Grace required minimal care, and Leon was old enough to lighten my workload. Otherwise, I would have lost my mind.

Mama enrolled Leon in a Catholic school at St. Stanislaus on 8th Street so that he could receive enough religious education to make his First Holy Communion. I went back to my father's name, Ziobro, because my parents lost the adoption papers and the public school would not accept me with Stepfather's family name without proof. In a way, I was happy to go back to my birth name, because I felt guilty for abandoning my Tatus's family name.

Over time, and with our parent's periodic guidance, Leon and I handled the day-to-day operations and maintenance of the entire sixteen-family apartment building. Each week we swept and washed the first floor. We washed the rest of the building's floors once a month. When Stepfather and Mama taught us how to operate the furnace, its maintenance and the rest of the chores became Leon's and my responsibility -after returning home from school, of course.

Except for the weekends, we saw little of our parents. Depending on how their relationship was faring at the time, not seeing them was sometimes a blessing. They usually argued about one thing or another. Between the arguments, Mama managed to find an office cleaning job. With Leon and me shouldering many of the daily janitorial duties, Stepfather branched out, taking small, better paying carpentry jobs. Stepfather was gone most of each day, and Mama left the house soon after Leon and I returned from school. Despite requests by girls from school to play in the afternoon, Mama absolutely forbade it. "There is too much work to do," Mama always said, no matter how often I asked.

Our family did have an oasis while we lived on East 11th Street. On the fifth floor of our building lived a fascinating Polish lady named Helena. Helena was a singer on a Polish radio station and a charity worker for the Polish Immigration Committee. Her guidance and support helped to ease the tensions of our new culture, our new language, and our new home. She helped our whole family get settled. She helped Stepfather find his janitorial job, and she helped us navigate the fast paced American way of life. Helena became our family's best friend and a lifelong advisor to me.

During the Christmas holidays, Helena took me to all of the department stores in Manhattan. We walked past the huge windows of each store and marveled at the holiday decorations, the ornate displays, and the glamorous mannequins. She introduced me to Macy's, Wanamaker's, Bloomingdale's and Gimbels. Sometimes we strolled past the window displays, only to stop for a moment or two if something caught our attention. Other times we'd step inside the stores for no other reason than to ride the escalators up and down. Still other times, we'd enjoy a brisk walk through the dry winter air among the hustling and bustling shoppers. Our noses were always red from the cold, but it didn't matter. Christmas in Manhattan was heaven, and Helena was my guardian angel.

Helena taught me how to crochet and showed me how to sew. Helena also taught me how to dress like a young metropolitan lady. She made me several flare skirts that were popular at the time. When nobody was looking, I loved to go up to the fifth floor where she lived and run down the stairs so fast that the skirt flew over my head. I thank God for the relief that woman brought to my life during those years. Her husband, Walter, was also an interesting man. He cared for pigeons that were kept on the roof top of our building in a huge cage. His pigeons served a valuable purpose during the war, delivering messages to and from Allied Forces. After the war they were returned to Walter, each with a diploma for service to our country. Unfortunately, when the landlord complained that the pigeons damaged the roof, they served their final purpose—as dinner one Sunday evening for Helena's family and friends. My time with Helena was never as long or frequent as I wanted.

During those years, my janitorial duties and household chores, the caring for my brother and sister, and my schoolwork were interspersed with the sound of Mama and Stepfather's arguing and irrational behavior. Despite the never-ending struggles in their relationship, our family grew with the additions of Elizabeth, Barbara, and Wesley. Our financial situation gradually improved. Stepfather found steady work as a carpenter, which allowed him to leave the life of a janitor and move the family to a better home. Together with Mama's salary, they were able to buy an eight-family apartment house at St. Ann's Avenue and 156th Street. I helped raise most of my brothers and sisters there, and developed a motherly bond toward each of them. That bond kept me from acting on a thought that frequently entered my mind: I needed to leave my parents' house. I grew tired of their yelling, screaming, threats, accusations, and even fistfights. I had enough of being their referee, while managing all of my other duties. I had to get some sanity in my life.

Unfortunately, the years of hearing Stepfather tell me that I wouldn't amount to anything affected my self-esteem. My poor self-image kept me there longer than I would have otherwise preferred. Eventually, however, I came to terms with my self-doubt and, at nineteen years old, moved out of their house. I moved to a boarding house with a single room and a kitchenette.

I missed my sisters and brothers terribly. I thought about them constantly during those days. I remember how, when I walked with them through the park, strangers approached me to remark at how strikingly beautiful they all were. And they were. What I missed most was the gentleness and kindness we exchanged with one another. The way they made me laugh. Their childlike purity. Their inner beauty. How I missed seeing them during those times! At first, my parents were furious at me. Although I knew, deep down, Mama understood, it took Stepfather much longer to accept my leaving. My relationship with him was strained for years. Over time, however, things did improve between us, but not between them.

They eventually bought a farm in Oxford, New Jersey. They had about twelve acres, a cow, a horse, some chickens, and a garden with cabbage, tomatoes, potatoes, and other vegetables. They even managed to buy a beat-up old car. In some ways, the farm lifestyle provided a nostalgic return to a typical Polish homestead. From Mama's perspective, the resources were thankfully more abundant. The farm also offered an opportunity for them to raise their children in a more family-friendly environment. Stepfather had a difficult time finding work in rural, western New Jersey, though. Any jobs that he did find couldn't come close to matching the wages he could earn in the city, so they agreed to keep the home on St. Ann's Avenue where he lived during the week while at work.

Mama had suffered what doctors believed was a nervous breakdown in Germany for which she sought almost no help. After a few years in Oxford, she was placed in the hospital and finally received the care that was well overdue. Her recovery was long and complex. She even received electric shock treatments. We'll never know how the deep, lasting scars of the war affected her personality and her mental state.

Through it all, Mama maintained a steadfast loyalty to the American soldier. One day, on a ride back to the farm, Mama saw a hitchhiking soldier wearing fatigues and carrying a large duffle bag. His shoulders slouched and his head hung low as he trudged along the two-lane, dusty road. The car was bursting at the seams with the entire family, but Mama pulled over anyway. There was no room for another person, but that fact didn't faze Mama. "Move over, kids! Basia, get on Grace's lap. Elizabeth, hold Wesley. Hurry, children! Hurry!" She later said, "With all that the American soldiers did for me, I'll never pass up an opportunity to help one of them."

Mama and the other children continued to work the farm. Stepfather visited from time to time. Unfortunately, the distance and the time apart did little to ease the tension between them. Finally, after years of battling, they were worn out. Stepfather and Mama divorced. At Mama's insistence, she stayed on the farm in New Jersey, and he kept the home on St. Ann's Avenue.

In later years, when the children were grown and with nobody left to maintain the farm, Mama retired to a small home in Florida. She eventually moved north again, to Pennsylvania to be closer to her children when her health began to fail. Even as she got on in years, she managed to make it back to Poland from time to time to stay close to her roots. Mama never spoke poorly about her mother or her siblings, despite how she was treated by some of them. Moreover, she assisted in bringing Babcia, all of her own siblings, and some of their families over to America. I cosigned some of those loans when Mama ran out of collateral to secure funds for their passage.

She had a soft spot in her heart for people in need, particularly those in search of a better life. On one of her trips back to Poland, she befriended a family in Ropczyce and ultimately sponsored one of them in their effort to come to America. Ultimately they settled in Toronto, where Mama visited them from time to time. She died on August 18, 1992, while attending the wedding of one of their family's children. She was seventy-six.

Stepfather had long moved on. He embarked on a new chapter in his life with a new family in New York. Despite their difficult marriage, when Mama died, he had only good things to say about her. I called to let him know that Mama had passed away. "She was a good woman," he said. "She was a good woman." To honor her life, although they had been divorced for many years, he paid for her monument at the cemetery. I gained a great deal of respect for Stepfather that day.

Dreams and flashbacks of the war haunt me, forcing me to remember all that we experienced. While on my own in New York, I encountered people who had similar experiences to mine, and worse. Some of them became lifelong friends. There was Wanda and Adela, whose mother and infant brother Ukrainian partisans in Poland killed with a knife. To finish the family off, the partisans torched their house. Luckily their uncle ran to their house, opened the door to let them out, and hid the young girls in the nearby stable until the terror subsided. Wanda was four and Adela was two.

Mama's friend Janina and her family were shipped to Siberia and ultimately Uzbekistan as forced laborers. Their living conditions were shocking, and the amount of nourishment they received was inhumane. Janina and her family were eventually separated, and she lost contact with them all. Later she went back to find some information about what happened to them. The government records that remained showed no trace that they even existed. Thousands of Polish people had similar experiences where their families were shipped to Russia and other far-away places without a trace. I think of how lucky Mama and I were, by comparison.

I think about those who perished in concentration camps, including some of the Jews who lived with us in Ropczyce. I wonder what became of them all. Did any of them survive? Those people must have shared the same big dreams as I did before their lives were cut short or changed forever. For those who did survive the torture and inhumanity, I can scarcely imagine how fresh the pain must be for them, even today.

For a long time after arriving in New York, I held a disdain for German people. I hated them for what they did to me, my whole family, and the world. I hated them for taking my childhood. I hated them for their deep abhorrent treatment and insensitivity toward Jews and Polish people. There's a great deal of effort involved in hating. It's always on your mind. It consumes you. If you let it, hatred can define who you are. After realizing that fact and taking stock of my life, I decided that it was not whom I wanted to be. It was not whom God wanted me to be. If I were going to move beyond the war and into the next phase of my life, I would need to put the hatred behind me. I didn't want to forget what happened, but I was not going allow my life to be defined by that hatred, so I chose to forgive. When I decided to let it go, I was surprised at how therapeutic it was.

I went on with my life. I married, raised a wonderful family, and have much to be thankful for. Long after my children were grown, I learned that while living in the slave labor camps our status as American citizens probably saved our lives. The Nazis knew that, regardless of their feelings toward any particular group, culture or nation, they would have to account for every documented American life, including ours. Despite what the labor camp bosses said to Mama, our citizenship is believed to have been the reason that Mama and I were never separated during our time in the slave labor camps. It also might explain why I was one of few slave labor camp children we ever saw there. Among other uncommon privileges we were granted, our citizenship is also believed to be the reason that, when exhaustion overtook Mama's ability to work, we were allowed to move from one camp to another instead of being shipped directly to a concentration camp. I feel lucky to be alive.

After all I've been through, I've finally reached the horizon I daydreamed about from the top of my cherry tree in Granice. As I look back and contemplate these past many years, I consider the things that matter most. I think of my parents. They were not perfect, but who is? They worked hard all their lives. They did the best they could, considering the circumstances into which they were thrust. They did not leave me a fortune or even a small dowry, but they left me a memory of many life lessons and a treasure of siblings, whom I love dearly. Despite all the struggles during and after the war, Mama and Stepfather somehow managed to instill a strong sense of family in all of us. For that I am most grateful.

BIBLIOGRAPHY

1. http://en.wikipedia.org/wiki/Shtetl
2. Redwald, Hugh. "From Counter-Reformation to Glorious Revolution," page 51. © University of Chicago Press 1992.
3. http://en.wikipedia.org/wiki/Galicia_(Central_Europe)
4. http://en.wikipedia.org/wiki/Ropczyce#cite_note-12
5. http://en.wikipedia.org/wiki/Galicia_and_Lodomeria
6. The Jewish Connection website. http://ajewishsoul.blogspot.com/2008/01/oy-veh.html
7. http://en.wikipedia.org/wiki/Battle_of_the_Bulge
8. http://www.historyplace.com/worldwar2/timeline/ww2time.htm#rhine
9. http://en.wikipedia.org/wiki/Nazi_crimes_against_ethnic_Poles
10. Moshe Lifshitz, Zionism." (תונויצ), p. 304